UNWRAPPING YOUR SPIRITUAL GIFTS

UNWRAPPING YOUR SPIRITUAL GIFT(S)!

How *you*, my fellow Christian, can identify what spiritual gift(s) you have received, operate in your gift(s), and give God glory.

William L. Garvin

TABLE OF CONTENTS

ACKNOWLEDGMENTS

Some of the definitions on the gifts of the Holy Spirit in chapters 4 and 5; have been taken partially from the book; *The Holy Spirit and His Gifts,* by Kenneth K. Hagin copyright 1974, Rhema Bible Church. Quotations taken from this book are italicized, with the page numbers included.

DEDICATION

To God, who has given His people, the unimaginable' gift of *Himself*, perfectly expressed in His Son, Jesus Christ, —our Lord and Savior—and His Holy Spirit, who empowers us to live in Christ Jesus.

To Beverly Joyce, my wife of fifty-plus years, who has walked with me, encouraged me, has suggested, has corrected, and has prayed with and for me throughout writing this book.

To the elders, ministers, and saints of God at Home Ministry Outreach Church in Gary, Indiana.

To my sisters, Armeca and Andrea, for their support and encouragement and to Pastor Joel Ombati, the leadership, congregation, and "orphanage," of the Home Ministry Outreach Church in Kesii, Kenya. {To all who read this book, please pray for Pastor Joel and the Kenyan church, that God will supply food, clothing, and the educational needs for the over fifty orphaned children who have come and are coming to them for help. There is a special need for food and sanitary water. If you wish to help, email pastor Joel at ombatijoel80@gmail.com.}

ABOUT THE AUTHOR

As a child in the 1950s and a teen in the late 1960s, I lived a conflicted life. I was born an American citizen, but forced to be a part of another nation separated from the opportunities of white America by skin color, white supremacy, and legalities.

I grew up listening to my father and grandfather's experiences while facing my own challenges with white America. My parents and the rest of the family attended church regularly. But as I grew into my late teens, I deduced that the Christianity that my parents believed was not truth. Clearly, it was unscientific and mythological, and those who seemed to really believe it acted *strange*. I often asked questions about creation and other Bible stories, but either got no answers or was told to "just believe." It seemed that Christianity was designed by white society to keep the blacks in America subservient, turning the other cheek, passive, and nonviolent. Nonviolence may have worked for the civil rights movement, but it did not stop the evil in the white people. And the foundation of this evil was their hypocritical, unscientific religion. This conclusion led me to consider myself an atheist; my morals were determined by what I judged to be right or wrong. Therefore, I believed I had a "right" to kill what had been trying to kill my people and me.

My oldest sister, Armeca, came to Christ in 1971 and felt led by the Lord to believe that if she separated herself from her family church, He (God) would save her family. Well truly, my other sister, Andrea; mother, Earnestine; and father, Macy, committed themselves solely to Jesus. Though I rejected everything Armeca and my family said, they prayed. In 1973, Jesus reached me.

To violently overthrow white people was still my game plan, but I was challenged by an in-law, "Have you ever really read the Bible?" My answer was, "No, but to get you out of this religious delusion you have, I will read it. I'm going to show you the myths, stupidity, unscientific errors, and racism that has deceived you." So, I did read it, and the "script was flipped" because God showed me in the Bible, that Jesus was *truth*. Convicted of my sin, I went to a midweek service at my sister's church. I prayed in repentance, went to my seat, and then I heard God say to me, "You don't have to hate anymore!" He cast out that spirit of hate, filled me with his Holy Spirit, and has kept me ever since. Praise God!

INTRODUCTION

For the gifts and the calling of God *are* irrevocable.
(Rom. 11:29)

The second chapter of the Book of Acts opens with an announcement of the exciting and amazing fulfillment of a promise given by God to the people of Israel. It reads, "and they were all filled with the Holy Spirit and began to speak with other tongues as the Spirit gave them utterance" (Acts 2:4). In explaining this phenomenon, the apostle Peter quotes from the book of the prophet Joel, where it says, "And it shall come to pass, in the last days, says God, that I will pour out My Spirit on all flesh; your sons and your daughters shall prophesy, your young men shall see visions, your old men shall dream dreams; and on My menservants and on My maidservants, I will pour out My Spirit in those days; and they shall prophesy" (Acts 2: 16 -18). Peter's application of these Scriptures from Joel, tells us that this pouring out of the Holy Spirit would last throughout "the last days."

We Are in the Last Days!

Let us continue reading Acts 2:38: "Then Peter said to them, 'repent, and let everyone of you be baptized in the name of Jesus Christ, for the remission of sins; and you shall receive the gift of the Holy Spirit. For the promise is to you and to your children and to all who are afar off, as many as the Lord our God will call.'" So, this promise is for everyone whom the Lord calls. If these words are true—and they are—we are living in an exciting, spiritually invigorating time for all those who have claimed Jesus as Lord over their lives. Now is the time that the prophetic words of Joel are still being fulfilled before our eyes.

The apostle Peter then continues to quote Joel, establishing some unorthodox happenings that will signal God's spiritual move during this era. Peter explains to the gathered people of Israel that they are visually seeing and hearing the authority and power that God, the Father, has placed in His resurrected Son, Jesus the Messiah (Christ). After all, Jesus had said, "all authority has been given to Me in heaven and on earth" (Matt. 28:18). Peter continues, "this Jesus, God has raised up, ... therefore, being exalted to the right hand of God, and having received from the Father, the promise of the Holy Spirit, He, (Jesus) poured out this; which you now see and hear" (Acts 2:32, 33).

This work of Jesus, to "baptize us in the Holy Spirit," had been declared by John the baptizer, and demonstrated by him as he immersed repentant Jewish believers in water. So, Jesus also would immerse believers—in the Holy Spirit. John had said, "I indeed baptize you with water, but one mightier than I is coming ... and he will baptize you with the Holy Spirit and fire" (Luke 3:16).

Question: Is being baptized in the Holy Spirit the same as receiving the Holy Spirit at salvation?

Good question!

It should be noted that after His resurrection the disciples of Jesus received the Holy Spirit when Jesus breathed on them, (John 20:22). I believe Jesus "breathed" on each of the 120 believers who were in the room on the day of Pentecost, in that they had each seen the Lord, been in His resurrected presence; and received the Spirit during the forty days before His ascension (Acts 1:2, 3). *Yet it was still necessary that all of them be baptized in the Holy Spirit ten days after His ascension.* I think this lets us know that we, who have accepted His salvation, can anticipate also receiving this outpouring—the baptism—of the Holy Spirit.

Question: Some have doubts; is it for every Christian?

Yes, I certainly believe that it is! That is one reason why this is written; so that you also will believe it. I believe that every Christian can and will receive this Holy Spirit baptism, unless doubt or fear diminishes your faith.

I do not want to hide our goals for your reading this workbook! I want you to know them plainly:

1. Our first goal is to convince, reason, and encourage you, from the Scriptures, to have faith and to receive the baptism of the Holy Spirit.

2. We will define sixteen spiritual gifts and what they do.

3. We will clarify their spiritual purpose, operation, and limitations.

4. Finally, we hope to help you identify the spiritual gift(s) the Holy Spirit has given you and suggest ways they can be activated in your life.

Another goal of our writing is to bring an understanding of the differences between natural gifts, spiritual gifts, and ministry gifts. The Scripture reads, "However, the spiritual is not first, but the natural and afterwards the spiritual" (1 Cor. 15:40).

Natural gifts are those that we are born with. Spiritual gifts are supernatural, and they are given when we are born again by the Holy Spirit.

Ministry gifts (aka callings) are where Jesus combines the spiritual gifts in several believers, empowering them to work together to fulfill His will, in nine arenas of ministry. It is these "callings" that will maintain and preserve the body of Christ until *His* return (Eph. 4:7–12; 1 Cor. 12:27–30).

The Bible records that because of ignorance and misunderstanding, the spiritual gifts, particularly tongues, had been abused by some Christians in the ancient city of Corinth. Its abuse had led to some services that seemed disruptive and uncontrollable. Yet, under certain guidelines, its use was encouraged (1 Cor. 14:39). Church historians have recorded that the use of tongues in the church seemingly died out. Yet, in times of great revival, it would seem to pop up again. Unfortunately, many denominational leaders, in a desire to keep our worship services done "decently and in order" (1 Cor. 14:40), have sought to find a scriptural way to delete "tongues" from the gift list. Undoubtedly our misunderstanding of God's purpose and use of tongues is at the heart of the controversy. But the question remains: "Is speaking in tongues really necessary for the twenty-first-century Christian?"

Therefore, in this writing, we are launching a special investigation on tongues: seemingly, the most maligned, ignored, and purposeless gift, for our present-day applications. Unless we understand what God is doing with tongues, it is difficult to see any practical use for it in our church ministries. I believe our Bible clearly shows the use for the gift of tongues, in times past, and our need for the gift today. But the Scriptures also point out that there are specific limitations on the use of tongues.

My hope is that by the time you finish reading this book, you will understand what the spiritual gifts are. You will know how to determine what gifts you have and how they can be accessed in your life. You will become aware of the Holy Spirit guiding you, as He uses the (gift)s in you to minister to others and edify yourself. Your spiritual gift will make you a more effective witness to the unsaved. Spiritual gifts aid you to share our living Lord by pinpointing the very "secrets of their hearts" (Rom. 14:25). Through the spiritual gifts of the Holy Spirit, the unbeliever is convicted and convinced that God is truly *in* you.

You

Must

Be

Born

Again!

CHAPTER ONE
YOU MUST BE BORN AGAIN

The New Testament, starting from Acts chapter 2, is full of descriptions of the miraculous nature of the 'Baptism in the Holy Spirit' and the spiritual gifts that He gives us. The operation of these gifts identifies the believers as being "like Jesus." They went from a fearful huddle of eyewitnesses of the resurrection of Christ, to boldly declaring Him as living to the very powers who had killed Him. The Holy Spirit used these gifts as *evidence*, forcing even their enemies to know that "they had been with Jesus" (Acts 4:18). Starting with the speaking in tongues (Acts 2:4), interpretation of tongues (Acts 2:11), teaching and exhortation (Acts 2:15–38), word of wisdom (Acts 2:39–40), word of knowledge (Acts 2:32), healings and miracles—listed as "signs" and "wonders" (Acts 2:43), gifts of giving, mercy, and service (Acts 2:45–46); all these gifts are displayed in this one chapter. And look at the outcome of this first-day outpouring of the Holy Spirit and his spiritual gifts—3,000 souls were saved.

The encouragement, excitement, and wonder of reading and hearing God displaying His power through His believers two thousand years ago is glorious. But, what is even more glorious is that *He is willing to do the same things through us today*. Yet, it does not seem to be that way with many in the Church.

It has been my experience that we eagerly tell new and old believers in Christ that they have been given a spiritual gift by the Holy Spirit. We encourage them to know more by reading the New Testament Scriptures that mention it (1 Cor. chapters 12–14; Rom. 12:3–8; 1 Peter 4:10–11). The believer's next questions are usually, "What is my spiritual gift?" And "How can I receive it?"

Spiritual gifts can only be received through God's spiritual methods. And everything that is genuinely of God, *starts* with Salvation and being filled with the Holy Spirit. Attempting to operate in spiritual things without following God's way (as revealed in the Scripture and by the Holy Spirit) has led to attempts to explain the gifts as natural and practical things we can do for our church, pastor, or ministry. The spiritual gifts of the Holy Spirit cannot be explained, received, or activated through purely natural or practical activities. The true gifts of the Holy Spirit are not obtained through ways and actions we can normally explain, understand, manipulate, and achieve. In Acts 8:12–23, the narrative mentions a man called a "believer" (Simon) who desired the spiritual gifts but wanted to receive them by paying for them. Yet the Scripture reveals his heart was not right to receive the baptism of the Holy Spirit. Before Holy Spirit baptism, God must clean our hearts, "Now we have received not the spirit of the world, but the Spirit who is from God, that we might know the things that have been freely given to us by God" (1 Cor. 2:12). Clean hearts come only by receiving true salvation through Christ Jesus.

The Holy Spirit is given to every true believer freely at salvation, residing in the human Spirit. It is when we are baptized in the Holy Spirit that He fills our total being, (spirit, soul, and body), with His presence. If we try to get the gifts before true salvation, we are relying on flesh and not the Holy Spirit. This reliance on the flesh can be extremely dangerous and detrimental, possibly opening us up to an evil spiritual realm without spiritual protection.

Therefore, those of us who are leaders; let us make sure we are not substituting church activities and natural explanations for the true biblical spiritual explanations. Let us ensure we are supplying the believer with the proper *biblical definitions*, so they may have confidence *to identify the prompting of the Holy Spirit*, as He introduces spiritual gifts into their born-again life (1 Cor. 12:1). Let us make time in our Christian church services where the believers can see "gifts" working in other more mature believers (1 Cor.11:1) and allow the believer to learn to exercise their gift under the watchful eyes of church leadership.

Our God is above the natural; so, too, are the gifts of the Holy Spirit (Isa. 55:8, 9). To have any chance of understanding His ways, we must come up to His level. How is that possible? Let us see!

First Things First: Before the Gifts We Must Personally Know the Giver

The Word of God, the Bible; quotes Jesus as saying, "You must be born again" to a man (Nicodemus) searching for answers (John 3:2). To be born again happens when the Spirit of life in Christ takes up residence inside our human spirit.

The eighth chapter of Romans gives us a brief preview of some of the spiritual events that should happen to everyone who professes to being 'born again'. In that chapter we are first informed (v. 9): "now, if anyone does not have the Spirit of Christ, (the Holy Spirit) he is *not* His." This is a foundational revelation for us—a person is not a Christian if the Holy Spirit does not dwell *in* him!

Fake News?

The presidential election of 2016 in the United States brought in a new phrase called "fake news." This implied that the various news outlets of TV, radio, internet, social media, and others were reporting facts, but were adding their *bias* to their reporting. This resulted in a coloring of the facts, leaving viewers or listeners to a wrong understanding. It was charged that the news media knew the truth but allowed these misconceptions to flourish, thereby allowing the public to believe a lie.

I believe a similar issue exists among many who profess to be Christian. Some honestly believe that they are Christian, but *in truth, they are not*. This discussion of receiving and operating with the spiritual gifts would be unattainable to them, even though they would possibly agree with what is being said. Therefore, I must challenge you that before we talk about spiritual gifts, are you certain that you are a Christian? Do you have the Holy Spirit living in you?

Traditional (or Cultural) Christianity

In the United States, according to responses given to the George Barna research group in 2016, it was estimated that about 73 percent of American adults claim to be Christians. According to Barna, 48 percent of that 73 percent of Americans are not Christians at all but are "post-Christians." This is a category for those who once professed, but now are unsure. That means less than half of Americans who say they are Christians, are really Christians *in name only*.

Again, according to Barna, only 34 percent of Americans claim to be born-again Christians. Yet, even of that number, only 9 percent of Americans understand what Christ's salvation had created them to be; not merely converts but *new creations*.

Why must we become new creations? Because we were born in sin from our mother's womb (Ps. 51:8) and under the law of sin and death (aka the law of Moses). The Scriptures declare that the law is "holy, the commandment right, just and good" (Rom. 7:12). The law is perfect, but those born in sin cannot obey it, for no matter how hard we try, we disobey it. The law is more than just how we commit unlawful acts. It is about how we think, contemplate, and desire. The book of James tells us if we disobey it in one point, we are condemned as if we broke all the commandments (James 2:10). We cannot please God by trying to work our way to Him. That is why "cultural" Christianity can be so deceptive. It makes you think that your "good works" make you right with God when, in reality, they do not."

Cultural deception may say, "We are Christians because we live in a Christian nation," but biblical truth says entire nations cannot be Christian because Jesus saves only *individuals* who commit and submit their complete loyalty to Him. They become citizens of the kingdom of God. (Important distinction: a nation can have true Christians living in it who—depending on the type of government that they live in—may affect the laws of the land to reflect some Christian principals, but ultimately secular governments will degenerate to "the course of this world" (Eph. 2:2).

Being born-again is a state of being that has nothing to do with what part of the globe you were born. It has nothing to do with being born of a special people, religious or political group (such as Jewish, Muslim, Hindu, Israeli, Republican, Democrat, White, or Black). Jesus says, "If *anyone thirst*, let him come to Me" (John 7:37).

Cultural Christianity deceives when it causes you to believe you are saved because you get a warm and satisfying *feeling* when you buy gifts on Christmas or give to the poor. Or because you attend church regularly, or give in the offering. Deception has crept in if you think that since your parents were "saved," you are also. After all, God has NO grandchildren, only 'children' of God. Some are deceived when they do not realize that salvation does not come from water baptism (though needful), taking communion, praying (though necessary), or even reading the Bible (though helpful). The salvation that results in the born-again experience does not come from anything we can do. It all is dependent on *what God did.*

Our part in this is merely one of receiving by accepting the results of the work Jesus did. We could do nothing. God chose to make the way back to Him, a demonstration of the depth of His love for us. He made the way—the only way!

The Blood Atonement

The concept of "sin" is not something made up by Bible thumping, hell-fire preachers. It is old; its entrance goes all the way back to God's perfect creation and the first humans. And sin's entrance with the disobedience of Adam, resulted in the curse of death to all his progeny. Thus, Adam; in his disobedience to God's commandment, brought death, and all its tendrils of decay, sickness, disease, depression, and more into God's perfect creation. And the most disturbing fact of this, he (Adam) transferred that sinful nature—the natural propensity to disobey God—to all born through human sexual intercourse. When Adam and Eve were expelled from the garden, they and their descendants were separated from God.

As mentioned earlier, sin introduced a different "nature" into Adam, and ultimately into all of us, a "nature" that corrupted Adam's perspective about God. He went from walking with God to hiding from God, from loving being in the presence of God to being afraid of God. This new nature prompted him to question God's motives and blame

God for causing his disobedience (Genesis 3). And that "nature" is with all humans today, embedded in our physical bodies. In the Scriptures, it is called "the flesh" or the "sinful" nature, and its life force is in our blood. This 'flesh' or 'sin-nature' works so powerfully in us that it makes it impossible to obey God. The prophet Isaiah said, "but your sins have separated you from your God, and your sins have hidden His face from you, so that He will not hear" (Isa. 59:2).

But God, reaching out to humanity, provided a way for those who would seek him to reach out to him: blood sacrifice, which was first done by God himself for Adam's sin (Gen. 3:21) and continued all though time until the death of Jesus. This demonstrated to us that the cost of sin was brutal, anguishing, and horrible. The Father, being perfect in justice, requires that all sin must be atoned, or paid for, either by the death of the sinner himself or by the death of an innocent substitute. God, (Yahweh) in speaking to Israel says, "for the life of the flesh is in the blood, and I have given it to you, upon the altar, to make atonement for your souls, it is the blood that makes atonement for the soul" (Lev. 17:11). Unfortunately, that meant that every time we sin, a blood sacrifice would have to be offered to cover that sin. The sacrifice of animals was only temporary, lasting at the most for the nation of ancient Israel- a year and for individuals only until the next time that they sinned. Not only that, some sins, such as murder, adultery, and rape could only be covered by the death of the person who did those crimes (Heb. 10:4).

As you can see, this system for eradication of sin is impossible to maintain; so is trying to satisfy God by our own methods. And what is worse is that even if a person could obey all these things, God's standard for us to be with Him is perfection like He is. The Scripture thunders, "all have sinned and fallen short of the glory of God." (Rom. 3:23).

That is the grim reality; now, here is the good news! Our loving God had a plan that He had made before He founded the universe (Eph. 1:3). He planned the "new birth" for humanity, predicated on accepting for ourselves God's sacrifice—not our sacrifice, but His sacrifice of perfect blood that was shed by His Son, Jesus Christ—that had the power to eradicate the sins of all individuals ever born or who would ever live (Heb. 10:14, 17).

The old Christian hymn says, "What can wash away my sin, nothing but the blood of Jesus."

Only the perfection of Jesus can stand in front of the Father (Hebrews 9:14). Jesus's shed blood, His death, and resurrection provided the payment *for all sin of all mankind for all time* (1 John 2:2; Heb. 10:14, 17). But Jesus did not need it for Himself, as He had no sin-nature—He was not born of human sexual intercourse nor committed any sin; He did not have to die at all. But Christ suffered and died to produce "grace" (John 1:17). This grace allowed the Father legal right to absolve, remit, and eradicate the sin of any soul who came to Him in Christ Jesus. That is why the Scripture says, "by grace you have been saved" (Eph. 2:8). Yet to be IN Christ Jesus this *grace must be possessed through faith.*

How can a person, be in Christ through faith? What does the Scripture mean by faith? A simple way of saying it is, having confidence and assurance that what God has said, and what Jesus has done for us, is true and we believe it. And then we *act on that belief* by repenting, receiving, and obeying what He has said for us to do (see Heb. 11:1).

Let's look at the spiritual steps to our salvation. God has said that we are all sinners. The Holy Spirit has convicted us of our sin condition (John 16:8), we respond to the Holy Spirit's conviction through what the Bible calls, godly sorrow (2 Cor. 7:9, 10), and we become repentant. *This conviction is the first work of the Holy Spirit in our lives* (See John 16:8,

9). He convicts us—making us truly sorrowful and appalled at our sinful state—we see ourselves as God sees us and abhor ourselves, recognizing we are sinners.

Yet we discover God's plan that will absolve us of all sin, and we believe that it is for us. Included in this glorious, "good news" is that God has also supplied the 'faith' necessary to believe and receive Him, (Rom.12:3). This faith that God supplies results in a response from the heart in reaching out to attain and believe what God has said to do (Rom. 10:6-13). Our faithful heart surrendering statement of repentance, confession, and loyalty to Christ, on our part, leads to God receiving us and the eradication of the records and memory of our sins on God's part. Romans 10:9 reads, "If you confess with your mouth, Jesus as Lord, and believe in you heart that God raised him from the dead, you will be saved." (NLT).

Counting the Cost (Luke 14:26, 27, 33)

Before we covenant ourselves to loyalty to Jesus through prayer and faith, we need to know what we are giving up. *You are giving up* all, as Jesus said, "if you want to be my disciple, you must (by comparison) hate everyone else; father and mother, wife and children, brothers and sisters, yes, *and even your own life*, otherwise you *cannot* be my disciple" (Luke 14:26 NLT).

When we declare Jesus as Lord, meaning he is God and Master, we must actively understand that we are surrendering ourselves to become His servants and disciples. This is an extremely important understanding. It gives us a clue of how we can be in Christ. The servant is the master's property—purchased by the master; the disciple lives as his Master lives. The sinful nature we received at birth and the sins we committed as we yielded to that nature were our personal sins. They belonged to us. We deserve to die and be cast in hell for those sins. But when we make Jesus our

Lord, we become His property *and all we have becomes His*. You see, our sins, become His sins. He became sin for us (2 Cor. 5:21). We no longer have sin. Since it now belongs to Him, His righteousness is imparted to us, and we can live as disciples to Him.

John 1:12 says, "But as many as received Him, to them he gave the right to become children of God, to those who believe in His name." If you have not received Him before, and even if you have, it's okay to do it again; receive Jesus as the Lord and savior of your life, right now. Pray right now in your own words or use this suggested prayer:

> Father, I repent of my sins against You. I ask you to forgive me. Lord, I receive for myself the sacrifice you made for me, in your Son, Jesus Christ. Today I receive His shed blood, suffering, and death as payment for my sins, and I thank You that Jesus is alive and living within me through the Holy Spirit. In the name of my Redeemer and Savior, Jesus Christ. Thank you and Amen.

> When you speak this, and believe it in your heart, you are saved. With that, you become engraved into the very body of Christ. And gloriously, the Holy Spirit Himself takes up residence inside your human spirit. Your body becomes God's temple, now—and this is truly glorious and unimaginable, but true—the very presence of God is placed inside you. (1 Cor. 6:19, 2 Cor. 4:7, 2 Cor. 6:16, Eph. 2:22, Romans 12:1).

> Welcome to the Family and Kingdom of God in Christ Jesus!

Praise Stop: Can you imagine the glory of this, that the God of the universe would invite you to be made righteous by exchanging your life for his Son Jesus and giving you the awesome privilege to be a part of the family of God? Praise our Lord and King forever! There is none like Him; besides Him, there is none else.

Salvation Continues: Growth

When a person receives Jesus, he becomes a believer not only in Jesus, but also a believer that the Bible is God's accurate, unfailing testimony of Jesus Christ. The newborn Christian has only one spiritual food, and that is the Word of God. It is water, milk, bread, and meat for all stages of Christian growth (John 1:1; 1 Pet. 1:25; Heb. 13:8; 1John 2:12–14).

Assurance

How can you know, and be assured, that you are now inhabited by God (born-again)?

We WANT to Worship, praise, and give thanksgiving to God

God makes us aware of His presence in our inner man by bringing rejoicing, thanksgiving, worship, and praise to fill our hearts as we come to understand God's redemption of our lives (John 17:13; Acts 8:8, 39).

We "sense" a need to fellowship with other believers.

We seek out other 'believers' for fellowship, growth, and encouragement. (1 John 1:7, Heb. 10:25.26).

We believe God's promises:

We are promised by God, who cannot lie, that we are being transformed and conformed to the image of Jesus. As we cooperate and walk in the Holy Spirit, He will do just that in us (see Rom. 8:29; 12:1, 2; 2 Cor. 3:18; Eph. 4:23, 24; 6:1, 2; Col. 3:7, 8).

We Become "God-Conscious," Meaning:

We, who used to love sin, are now offended by it, even when we see it in ourselves. Repentance and receiving forgiveness (from God) sparks in us an awareness of our need to forgive others. Do not be surprised that you become more aware of sin than ever before. Remember His Word: "If we confess our sin, He is faithful and just to forgive our sin and clean us from all unrighteousness" (1 John 1:9). In cleansing our inner man, our sins must be brought to the surface of our conscience, so we become aware of them and repent, receiving God's forgiveness and cleansing. Remember, we are assured He dwells in us because He is transforming us from the inside out. (Romans 12:2, Rev. 3:20)

The Voice of God (the Holy Spirit) Becomes Clearer to Us

We hear His voice better, enabling us to choose the right and reject the wrong (Heb. 1:9). The born-again believer no longer is controlled by sin, no longer forced to live a sinful lifestyle. The believer is set free to choose to live in a way pleasing to God. (John 8:36, Romans 6:14)

We *Can* Renew Our Minds

God has saved our spirit. Now, we can renew our minds (souls) by reading, studying, and relying on the promises of the Word of God. We are to turn our will and thinking toward that we have been given, the mind of Christ (1Cor. 2:14–16; Phil. 2:5).

Water Baptism

Water baptism is one of the first things we do in being obedient to Christ, identifying ourselves as His obedient subjects, boldly bearing His name, and openly declaring He is our Master and Lord (Matt. 28:19; Mark 16:16; Acts 19:5). Water baptism is our picture to the outside world that Jesus has come in, and we want the world to know it. It symbolizes our death and burial to the old life and our bold declaration of complete surrender to His Lordship over our lives. (See Rom. 6:3, 4; Col. 2:11, 12; 1 Pet. 3:21.)

Water baptism is also a symbol of Holy Spirit baptism, where our Lord Jesus Himself (not a human believer) is the baptizer and the water symbolizes the Holy Spirit. Baptism in the Holy Spirit is the *one* baptism that is referred to in Ephesians 4:3. (See also Acts 10:44–45; Heb. 6:2.)

Remember the Barna Research we referenced earlier? Now, having read all of this, are you a repented, born-again disciple of Jesus Christ? Is he truly Lord of your life? If so, when we use the term Christian in this writing, we are talking about you.

Holy Spirit Baptism:
Unwrapping Your Gifts

CHAPTER TWO

THE HOLY SPIRIT AND OUR BAPTISM BY JESUS, INTO HIM

The promise of God is the infilling of the Holy Spirit to every true believer (Acts 2:17; Joel 2:28–32). But the tangible evidence of His reality comes as the Holy Spirit makes His presence known in our inner being. Jesus, in telling his disciples how they would know that the Holy Spirit would be present in them, even though they would not *see* Him, says, "And I will pray the Father, and He will give you another Helper that He may abide with you forever. The Spirit of truth, whom the world cannot receive, because it neither sees Him nor knows Him. But you shall know Him because He dwells with you and shall be in you also." (John 16:16, 17).

The Intimacy of "Knowing"

To 'know' someone, scripturally, is not just being aware of their existence or to hear about them from others. It implies an intimate and personal knowledge of them. Most of us are aware of the phrase, "Adam knew Eve his wife, and she conceived" (Gen. 4:1). It is the same with the Holy Spirit: His purpose is to reproduce in us the likeness (or holiness) of God so we will be able to display His holiness in our everyday living. Before

His entrance into our dormant human spirit, we were spiritually dead in trespasses and sin, but His entrance (with our salvation) brings eternal life and changes us profoundly. His presence is the seal of God's ownership of us and our certainty of heaven (2 Cor. 1:22; Eph. 1:13–14; 4:30). Through His intimate knowledge of us, the lost personal communication between us and God is restored. When He, the Holy Spirit, takes up residence in you, you will know it because He is dwelling in your inward being; being born-again means that you will start to have new spiritual experiences. Jesus, through the agency of the Holy Spirit, will start communicating on a personal level.

New Ears to Hear the Holy Spirit Speaking (Luke 8:8; Rev. 2:7, 11, 29)

With your new birth, you get new ears, spiritual ears. This is given to you to discern and know God's voice. Jesus said, "My sheep hear my voice" (John 10:27). There are many voices that may speak to us. We have our own thoughts, we have the outside world, we have communication from our family and friends, and—I say this to warn you—even voices of demonic spirits. How then, can we know when it is the Holy Spirit speaking?

We are to test the spirits because many false voices are speaking (1 John 4:1).

- The Holy Spirit will always confess the reality of Jesus as being fully human and fully God (1 John 4:2; 5:6; Acts 2:36).

- The Holy Spirit will never contradict the written Word of God (John 4:24; 6:63).

- The Holy Spirit speaks the words of Jesus to us (John 15:27).

- He, the Holy Spirit, will teach us all things (John 14:26).

- The Holy Spirit leads and guides us (John 16:13).

- The Holy Spirit enables us to discern truth from lies (1 John 2:26–27).

- He will testify of Jesus (John 15:26).

- He will tell us things to come (John 16:13).

- He will glorify Jesus (John 16:14).

- The Holy Spirit causes us to be assured and confident of His presence in us and that Jesus has paid for all our sin. (See 1 John 3:24.)

Praise Stop: Blessed be the Lord, our God and King who would honor us with His very presence inside our inward being. Thank You, O sovereign Master for living on the inside of us and calling and making us a temple for You to dwell in. This is too wonderful for me to comprehend, that You, the God who created all matter, space, time, and dimensions, would choose to live in our mortal bodies. In Your great wisdom, You have chosen to do this, and it is marvelous in our eyes. Thank you, thank you, thank you! Amen.

His presence and work in you are also displayed and seen by others who view your life from outside, displayed by the fruit of a changed life. Love, joy, peace, longsuffering, kindness, goodness, faithfulness, self-control will begin to be developed and displayed in your lifestyle. (Galatians 5:22).

The Baptism in the Holy Spirit

We have been assured that all Christians have received the Holy Spirit when they are saved. We have all been given authority to be sons of God, but we have been also promised '*Power*'.

There appears to be a difference between *receiving* the Holy Spirit and the baptism *in* the Holy Spirit. I say this because Jesus, after His resurrection, appeared to several of the disciples and said to them, "Peace to you, as the Father has sent me, I also send you. And when He had said this, He breathed on them, and said to them, *"Receive the Holy Spirit*, if you forgive the sins of any, they are forgiven them. If you retain the sins of any, they are retained" (John 20:21–23). Note: there was no work, no waiting, not even prayer necessary to receive this forgiveness. They merely breathed in and received. I believe at this point; they became the world's first born-again Christians. The Holy Spirit did not come upon them; He was received *IN* them. With that reception, Jesus made it clear that they had also received authority.

In the United States, each state has police officers with authority to stop fifty-three-foot-long (16.1 m) semi-trucks driving 70 miles an hour (112.6 kmh), on the expressways and toll roads. Their authority does not physically stop these big rigs from rolling. Obviously, no police officer could stick out his hand and bring that truck to a stop. Yet those eighteen-wheelers do stop when the trooper says so. The drivers of these massive freight haulers know *what and who backs up police authority.* State police authority is backed up by the resources of the entire state government. Not obeying that officer brings down more police, pursuit, weapons fired, capture, imprisonment, and judgment. So long as the truck drivers operate on the side of the authority, they experience the help, safety, peace, and order that the authority provides; if they are against the authority, it will carry out the penalty of fines, punishment, and jail time. *That power behind* the authority is what causes the truck drivers to stop.

We who are born-again have received the inward presence of the Holy Spirit through Jesus Christ. We have been given authority. This authority is not just to one or several denominational groups but to all His disciples worldwide. We are authorized to preach this gospel of God's forgiveness through Jesus Christ and to preach that there are eternal consequences of retaining your sins by rejecting God's offer. Through being in Christ, we have also gained authority over those spirits in the kingdom of darkness (Eph.1:22; 2:6; James 4:7). Our authority is backed up by the resurrected Jesus Christ, His blood, His Name, His Word, and all the spiritual forces of His kingdom.

The disciples received the Holy Spirit and authority to preach and warn, yet they were ordered to wait until they received the promise of the Father (Acts 1:4). Jesus had mentioned this promise several times, as recorded in the New Testament. In Luke 24:46–49, Jesus says to the disciples, "thus it is written and thus it is necessary for the Christ to suffer and to rise from the dead the third day; and that repentance and remission of sins should be preached in His Name to all nations, beginning at Jerusalem. And you are witnesses of these things. Behold, I send the promise of my Father upon you, but tarry in the city of Jerusalem, until you are endued with power from on high."

In the New Testament we have translated three Greek words into the English as the word, *power.* I do not read any form of the Greek language, classical, koine, demotic, or modern, but biblical scholars have provided us tools that I believe can help us understand the purpose of the baptism *in* the Holy Spirit.

To do this, I am using *Young's Analytical Concordance to the Bible,* by Robert Young, (Hendrickson Publishers). The three Greek words are *exousia,* meaning "privilege, authority"; *dunamis,* meaning "ability"; and *kratos,* meaning "strength."

The Scripture references that use *kratos* all denote divine power. The references that use *exousia* denote authority, which I take to mean a trust and assurance in the ability or power of someone else who has authorized them. And finally, *dunamis*—which is, by the way, where we get our word, *dynamite*—denotes the actual ability to do anything.

The receiving of Christ as our Savior gives us authority, especially over the demonic realm. But the baptism *in* the Holy Spirit is needed because it gives us abilities—power—through the operation of spiritual gifts, enabling us to do God's will and act as agents of the kingdom of God. It gets the world's attention to know that God is in us for His truth. The baptism of the Holy Spirit is God sharing His divine power (*kratos*) and trusting us to use it for His glory.

Benefits of the Baptism *in* the Holy Spirit:

The experience of being baptized in the Holy Spirit is God's fulfilment of His promise to Abraham, saying, "in Him— (His "seed," Jesus)—all nations of the earth will be blessed. The baptism of the Holy Spirit is the Father's special blessing for all the believers in Christ (Luke 24:49; Acts 1:5; 10:41).

The baptism *in* the Holy Spirit is *received by faith* before it may be felt or experienced. What I mean by this is that we move forth in what God's Word says will happen before it may visibly happen. Because God has promised it, we thank Him for it, even though it may not be a reality in our life at that time. Be assured that God will immerse you in His Spirit in due time. Consider the baptism to be God's initiation into you working for Him in the kingdom. Through the door of Holy Spirit baptism, we are privileged to be used of God as He ushers us into a small part of His divine power, and ability. The baptism gives us a yielded heart, enabling Him to affect our whole being: spirit, soul, and body. The Holy Spirit is enabled to flow through you to accomplish the kingdom purposes in our earth.

There is a difference in the work of the Holy Spirit in salvation and His work on us at the baptism in the Spirit.

In our salvation, we receive the Holy Spirit inwardly. The Holy Spirit, who is in us, authorizes us to operate in the role of priest under our High Priest—we are now assured of our prayers being heard because of our relationship to Jesus Christ (Heb. 4:14–16; 1 Pet. 2:5, 9; Rev. 1:6; 5:10). We are to "grow in the knowledge of Jesus," "preach the good news," and exercise our authority over the enemy (Luke 10:19; James 4:7; Col. 2:15). But note: a person may be authorized but not actually *able* to overcome and do it.

But with the baptism *in* the Holy Spirit comes the urging and *empowerment* to overcome the works of the enemy. Though it is true that we *were* sinners saved by grace; with the baptism *in* the Holy Spirit, our confession of who we are changes. We see ourselves as what God declares us to be: children of God, and saints of the Most High, practicing righteousness on a regular basis. We *receive more grace* whereby we are enabled to walk after the Spirit and not fulfill the lusts of our flesh (Heb. 4:16; Gal. 5:16; Rom. 6:12; 8:4). We may stumble in sin, but as the Holy Spirit leads us to repentance, we are able to respond and to be cleansed of all unrighteousness; then we are able to continue our walk in the Lord (1 John 1:9; 3:7–9). We begin to see signs of God's miraculous power everywhere we look. Our faith increases to expect to be used of God. We begin to see and overcome the lusts of the world system. We are enabled, through believing prayer, to live a life pleasing to God and to "put to death the deeds of the body." And, most importantly, we are empowered to share a bold witness of Jesus, regardless of circumstances. Many of these visible evidences are seen in the Church and by those of the outside world.

The Scriptures tell us about who is eligible to receive the baptism—it is called the promise, "then Peter said to them, 'repent, and let everyone of you be baptized in the name of Jesus Christ, for the remission of sins, and you shall receive, the gift, of the Holy Spirit.'"

When you received Jesus at salvation, the Holy Spirit came inside your human spirit. Through salvation He embedded His spiritual gift(s) in your born-again human spirit. It is the baptism in the Holy Spirit that allows those gifts to be readily perceived and acted out in your soul, and body. Thereby allowing you to spiritually build up yourself, other Christians, and even those in the outside world.

Receiving Holy Spirit baptism starts with prayer, but it must be faithful, expectant prayer. (The Father has already sent His Spirit on the earth, so no "tarrying" is necessary.) "*But* let him ask in faith, with no doubting. For he who doubts is like a wave of the sea, driven and tossed by the wind. For let not that man suppose that he will receive anything from the Lord. He is a double-minded man, unstable in all his ways" (James 1:6–8). You cannot receive the baptism when doubting whether it is biblical, right, or necessary. Some denominations teach against the outpouring of the Holy Spirit and His evidence (supernatural gifts) in our present day. Some tee- ter close to blasphemy in believing it is not of God or implying it may be demonic. You must resolve this issue in your sanctified conscience. Read the Scriptures, be assured that it is for you, and you will receive.

The time has come for your infilling. Let's take steps! Some important things to do:

Take more time in seeking the Lord, increase your prayer, and especially your praise times at home—many saints are filled at home in private prayer. Strongly desire the spiritual gifts of God (1 Cor. 14:1, 39).

As you asked for salvation, ask for the baptism by Jesus in the Holy Spirit! Receiving the baptism of the Holy Spirit is the initial step of God's ena- bling us to respond to his prompting by the Holy Spirit. God is adding to your authority the power (ability) to bring the things of the Spirit of God into our dimension.

Everything that is given by God must be received by—or mixed with—faith. To understand what I mean, look at Jesus's statement in Mark 11: "therefore I say to you, "whatever things you ask, when you pray, believe that you receive them, and you will have them" (Mark 11:24). When you pray for the infilling, thank God for giving you his baptism before there is any evidence. Because you know that God has already answered your prayer, begin to use your mouth to speak words of praise and worship, and when you run out of words (and sometimes before), expect God to use your mouth and tongue, to speak in one of three ways:

An 'inward utterance' – discernable outwardly as *moaning or groaning* (Rom. 8:15- 26) -that will seem to erupt out of your heart. Jesus had said, "out of your belly, shall flow rivers of living water" John 7:38 (KJV); Isa. 12:2-6). The Holy Spirit is overcoming our 'flesh' enabling HIM to intercede in prayers through us.

An unknown tongue: words spoken that seem and sound foreign to you—not in your native language or language that you have learned or even understand (Acts 2:4; 19:6). Prepare your hearts through songs of psalms and hymns (Eph. 5:19; Col. 3:16). Express in your native language words of praise, focusing your heart, mind, and soul on God, His attributes, His glory, might, power, and love. Read Psalm 34:1–8 as if you had written it yourself. In receiving the baptism, some have initially experienced difficulty in talking or even to seem to stutter. It may be that the Holy Spirit is gaining control of your tongue to forge spiritual songs and praise through your lips. You will taste and see, as the Lord pours out His Spirit on you. Open your mouth, breathe in then out, and began to speak. It may sound like baby talk (Rom. 8:15), but the language will mature as you continue worshiping in spirit. (Please note, many have received the baptism with the evidence of speaking in tongues in other different ways. Speaking in an unknown tongue, is one of the chief scriptural signs of Holy Spirit baptism. Some believers have experienced this once and have gone on not to speak again. But this sign is the door opener to all the other gifts.)

And third, *a Prophetic Utterance: speaking the words of God with unusual boldness* (Acts 4: 29-31). This usually occurs when you are under intense pressure by others attacking your confession or life of faith. Jesus had said, "therefore settle in your hearts not to mediate beforehand on what you will answer, for I will give you a mouth and wisdom which all your adversaries will not be able to contradict or resist (Luke 21:14, 15). These words, feelings, and actions will seem to rush out of you, as a "prophetic" utterance, in your native tongue.

If you have a spirit-filled overseer, elder, or pastor, have them lay hands on you to impart the infilling of the Holy Spirit (Acts 19:6; 2 Tim. 1:6). You will be filled with the evidence of His presence. Remember, God is most willing to fill you with His Spirit.

Jesus said, "ask and it shall be given, seek and you shall find, knock and the door will be opened to you. For everyone who asks, receives, and he who seeks, finds, and to him who knocks, it will be opened" (Luke 11:9, 10), and "how much more will your heavenly Father, give the Holy Spirit to those who ask him?" (Luke 11:13).

Receive the Holy Spirit now.

First

natural

then

Spiritual

CHAPTER THREE

NATURAL GIFTS, SPIRITUAL GIFTS, AND MINISTRY GIFTS

Natural gifts are different from spiritual gifts, but both are used in ministry gifts. Now that you are filled with the Holy Spirit, we can talk about these spiritual gifts that you have received.

The Importance and Necessity of the Holy Scriptures, the Bible

As we have stated before, the Word of God (translated from the original languages and texts in ancient Hebrew, Aramaic, and koine Greek) and the Holy Spirit will never contradict each other. It is He, the Holy Spirit, who moved holy men of old to write the Scriptures (2 Pet. 1:21). We will use the Scriptures to confirm and explain Scripture as we search out a fuller understanding of each gifting category.

Holy Spirit baptism results in certainty of the inerrancy of Scripture. With salvation and the baptism in the Spirit, the Bible becomes concrete truth for us. It has been delivered to us through millennia of attack on its historicity, veracity, and it has proven to be factual, verifiable, and accurate *truth* in every generation. It has been meticulously watched over by the Lord Himself, *for it is His revelation of Himself—His purposes and plans for all humanity.* It is God's precious gift, and tool, allowing us to span from our physical dimension into God's spiritual dimension and see how He plans to use us. He implants spiritual things in us, so that they, the spiritual things, may be brought out to our physical realm. The holy Scriptures, (the Word of God) gives us the foundation to help us to know the workings and promptings of the Holy Spirit in our lives (1 Pet. 1:22, 23).

Let us investigate the difference between natural gifts, ministry gifts, and spiritual gifts.

What are natural gifts, (talents)?

The capabilities given to us through our physical bodies from our ancestors.

Where did our ancestors get them?

They were given to our ancestors by God, via Adam and Eve.

When did that happen?

In the beginning, on the sixth day of creation, about 300 generations ago. (See Gen. 2:26–31.) Adam and Eve are declared by God that they were made in God's image, I believe this denotes them as being like God in their whole, tripartite being—body, soul, spirit (1 Thess. 5:23). They were given these natural gifts to rule over God's creation.

The fall of Adam and Eve (Genesis 3) resulted in death, specifically, the meaning of the word *death* was "in dying you shall die." Death is a process of continual downgrading until nothing retrievable is left. With the fall, Adam and Eve's perfect bodies no longer could transfer perfect replicas of their "savant genius" to their descendants. Death caused errors through mutations in the copying of the DNA, so through each successive generation some inherent skills were lost. But even the curse could not stop these inborn talents and skills from enabling humans to rule the earth. Genesis 4:17–22, gives us a brief history of this innate intelligence and skill that developed in the pre-flood society.

Cain created a city, resulting in a trade and barter economic system (Gen. 4:17). Jabel developed animal husbandry (v. 20). Jubal orchestrated the making of musical instruments and the skill to play them (v. 21). Jubal-Cain and his sister Naamah are credited with the discovery of foundry and metallurgy technology, producing bronze and iron for tools and weapons (v. 22).

Natural gifts were given to us to do work in the earth. They can be sharpened through training, exercise, education, and mentoring by those more experienced. Natural gifts include more than just our physical and mental abilities but also language, laughter, singing, and music. Some natural talents are sometimes mistaken as spiritual gifts, in that they affect our emotions and moods.

Natural talents are designed to make us aware of the image of God that is in us. We relish our power to create, think, and reason, which God uses to cause us to realize we did not, and could not, create ourselves (Ps. 100:3; Rom. 1:20). We rejoice in the strength, adaptability, and flexibility of our physical bodies, which testifies to us that we "are fearfully and wonderfully made" by God (Ps. 139:14). The massive range of our emotions are expressed through laughter, crying, grief, anger, compassion, and more, all reflecting to us that God also has feelings and that His feelings are concerned about us. Language is our door of communication to ourselves, to others, and to God.

Singing, dancing, and music are natural activities that affect all humans. They can control and regulate our mood from exuberance, to relaxed, and all the way down to depressive. Singing, dancing, and music are all used often by the "world" to manipulate our feelings. But God has given these natural abilities to help focus our conscious and unconscious state of mind (or mood) to have genuine feelings of joy and happiness on remembering the qualities of God's nature (His love, grace, peace, joy, power, and goodness) and a heartfelt exuberance in expressing His greatness to others. Singing and music further allow us to express our excitement that we can approach Him in repentance and praise. They can be used to set an atmosphere, allowing our conscience to be pricked, exposing our need for God.

"The world rejects God's purposes for these natural gifts and attributes these abilities to idols of self-worship, evolution, and demonic sources (1 Rom. 1:21-28)

Personal note: In our present day, the lies and deceptions of the "religion of Evolution" teaches that for nearly a million years 'archaic' humans wandered our globe as hunters and gatherers grunting to develop language and stumbling upon fire. And then, after 990,000 years, developed some primitive civilizations. This is taught in our schools as fact, but it is a fairytale, mythology created in the minds of men who have rejected the sovereignty of God, for make believe. The religion of Evolution is not science but a satanic attempt to destroy faith in the truth of the Scriptures. At one time I also believed it, but through the help of several Creation Ministries, and personal research, I found "Evolution" to be "the emperor that has no clothes."

Yet for spirit-filled believers, natural gifts are our first steps in reaching for God. Bible examples of singing and music, setting the stage for true prophetic giftings are King David in his psalms, and the prophet Elisha (see 2 Kings 3:15).

What Are Ministry Gifts?

The ministry gifts are listed in Ephesians 4:11 as: apostles, prophets, evangelists, pastors, and teachers. And, in 1Corinthians 12:28, other ministry gifts are added: miracles, healings, helps, administrations, and tongues. All these ministries, or callings, are for "equipping the saints for the work of ministry and for the edifying of the body of Christ." Although each ministry gift has its overall emphasis, they each have a *different grouping of spiritual gifts to do their job*. The ministry gifts are what our Lord Jesus has given to his church to maintain its existence and function through over 2,000 years and on until the return of Christ. However, all that they do is beyond the scope of this writing.

What Then Are the Spiritual Gifts?

The "spiritual gifts" are pictured in the Old Testament.

When we became born-again our loving Father betrothed us to his Son, by giving us His Holy Spirit (like an engagement ring), assuring us to be the bride of Christ at the marriage supper of the lamb, (Rev. 19:7-9). The spiritual gifts are the demonstration that our Father has paid the *bride-price*.

In Genesis 24, we have the narrative of Abraham's servant searching and finding a wife for Isaac. He was sent back to Padan –Aram (Syria) to find this wife. The servant prayed for God's guidance through specific signs so that he would know that he had found the perfect wife for his master's son. He found Rebekah. He knew she was the right one because God answered all the stipulations of his prayer. The servant then paid to her the *bride-price*—gifts given to her, letting her know she would marry into wealth and blessings.

The gifts of the Spirit are the Father's bride-price paid to us at our betrothal (salvation), before the actual marriage. But, unlike the valuable material gifts given to Rebekah, these are spiritual gifts, and they are extremely more valuable, being spiritual things.

41

Why Do We Need These "Spiritual Gifts" Operating in Our "Church" Services?

With the Holy Spirit's infilling, spiritual gifts will begin to sprout to each believer. These spiritual gifts are to enable you to:

- Fulfill God's divine purpose for you in His body (the church)

- Allow us to learn that as we work in spiritual unity, we may see a miraculous result

- Build up (edify) the members of Christ's body

- Supply believers with the power to effectively use our weapons of warfare to overcome the demonic kingdom that controls this world

- Demonstrate the power of God, convincing and convicting the world of its need for Jesus and making the world know that Christ is truly in us.

In summary:

Spiritual gifts are unique insights and abilities given directly by the Holy Spirit to individual believers, allowing them to glorify God in their personal witness of Jesus, edify (build up) themselves, and love each other as Christ has loved them (1 Cor. 12:7, 11; 1 Pet. 4:10, 11).

Clarifying the Spirit Realm

Because we live in an age where the term, *spiritual*, can be very confusing, we must have some quality control to know the "spiritual" from the holy true God, and the false "spiritual world" of deception. First Corinthians 2:13 gives us a standard we are to work by: "these things we also speak not in words that man's wisdom teaches, but which the Holy Spirit teaches, comparing spiritual things with spiritual."

Being born-again, we are spiritual people, but we must grow to rely on our born-again spiritual nature. We are only accustomed to our natural being (flesh) to make our day-to-day living decisions. *The work of the Holy Spirit is to train us to think spiritually*, so we will act spiritually. *The spiritual gifts are God's design to bridge us to act with the mind of Christ* (1 Cor. 2:16; Rom. 12:2).

How Then Do We Compare Spiritual Things with Spiritual Things?

The Holy Spirit will give us an inward witness, in our sanctified human spirit. A sense of peace and assurance in our inner man (John 14:27; 16:33).

The holy Scriptures will verify that witness: "all Scripture *is* given by inspiration of God, and *is* profitable for doctrine, for reproof, for correction, for instruction in righteousness," (2 Tim. 3:16). Jesus said, "the words that I speak to you are spirit and they are life" (John 6:63).

The gathered body of Christ (the local church) will further confirm that witness. The fellowship you attend is Christ's spiritual body: the elders, overseers, leaders, and fellow saints help judge spiritual gift operation.

Jesus says in Matthew 18:16, "by two or three witnesses let every word be established."

Testing the Spirits

> Now concerning spiritual gifts, brethren, I do not want you to be ignorant...therefore, I make it known to you that no one speaking by the Spirit of God, calls Jesus accursed. And no one can say, Jesus is Lord, except by the Holy Spirit. (1 Cor. 12:1–3).

Any spiritual message, thought, impression, or implication that says Jesus is not the Son of God, that word is not from God. And it is blasphemy to curse Jesus or to use Jesus's name as a curse. Not only that, only by the Holy Spirit can a person honestly declare the deity of Jesus "that Jesus is Lord."

Now that we have the guidelines to know the Holy Spirit derived spiritual things, let us continue to read.

> There are diversities of gifts but the *same Spirit*. There are differences of ministries but the *same Lord*. And there are diversities of activities, but it is the *same God* who works all in all. (1 Cor. 12:4)

It appears that the imparting of the "spiritual things" to the body of Christ is a work of the Godhead (Father, Son, Spirit).

Notice also, the terms for the responsibilities of each member of the Godhead:

The spiritual gifts— the Holy Spirit.

The ministries—Jesus Christ.

The diversities of activities—Father.

Let us look more closely at these significant words in verse 4 and see why they are important.

> *Gift,* from the Greek, *charisma;* English meaning "grace, favor, kindness."

> *Ministries,* from the Greek, *diakonia* (where we get our word, *deacon*); English meaning "to serve, administer, manage, direct, act of dividing."

Diversities, Greek, *diatresis;* English meaning "diverse, parting or distribution."

Activities/operations, Greek, *energema;* English meaning "energy, inworking."

The Holy Spirit gives to each individual believer the charisma—the spiritual gifts. These gifts are necessary to empower us for personal edification, worship, and prayer. By giving different gifts to individual believers, He allows our spiritual gifts to mesh with the gifts in other saints.

Our Lord Jesus divides out and manages how these spiritual gifts, which are given by the Holy Spirit, are brought together in the "right mix" to develop a person or group of persons to become a ministry (an apostle, prophet, pastor, teacher, evangelist, healings, administration, etc.) who provides service to the church.

God the Father distributes and energizes the gifts given by the Holy Spirit and operates within the ministries constructed by Jesus, to continually progress the church into the glorious bride of Christ throughout the days of the church on the earth.

I think an analogy using food could possibly further clarify this: Just suppose I wanted to feed my family. But to do this, they must have two fully nutritious meals each day: (let us call the morning meal breakfast, and a fully nutritious evening meal, dinner).

The terms *breakfast* and *dinner* would correspond to the ministry gifts given by Jesus, our Lord.

To make up these meals, I have available cereal, eggs, sausage, steak, broccoli, green beans, fish, milk, toast, jelly, syrup, and biscuits (these food items correspond to the gifts given to individuals by the Holy Spirit.) Some breakfasts might be composed of cereal and milk, and other breakfasts would require a greater mix of various ingredients. The same mixing would be necessary for the dinner meal. But the overall result is that the family would receive the necessary nutrition to energize the entire body; this corresponds to the Father's overall purpose to sustain and expand the Church.

To summarize our understanding of the differences: *spiritual gifts* are given to individuals by the Holy Spirit (see 1 Cor. 12:4, 8–11; Rom. 12:6–8). Jesus takes the gifted believers, installing them in His *ministries.* The Father uses the ministries, combining and dispensing them to oversee, administer, discipline, and build the Church, spreading the gospel worldwide.

Classification

Limitations

Controls

CHAPTER FOUR

CLASSIFYING THE SPIRITUAL GIFTS AND THEIR CONTROLS

A cknowledgment: some definitions on the gifts of the Holy Spirit have been taken partially from the book, *The Holy Spirit and His Gifts,* by Kenneth Hagin, copywrite 1974, Rhema Bible Church. Some of his conclusions I have not quoted directly, but where many of my conclusions agree with his, I have given the page number of this source book.

What Must Control Our Use of the Spiritual Gifts?

LOVE—operated through *faith and hope*

The spiritual gifts are overseen through one primary principal: "*agape*"— God's kind of love. *Agape* provides the parameters for the operation of the spiritual gifts. The entire chapter 13 of 1 Corinthians is written to establish God's Love as the overarching purpose of all the gifts. The spiritual gifts are to be demonstrated through patience, kindness, humility, without competitiveness, holding no grudges, speaking, and working these gifts with more concern for others than for ourselves. As we move forward in our individual giftings, they result in rejoicing in what is good and enable us to see evil and reject it.

When the gifts are operated under the control of love, they are *activated* through two means: hope and faith.

Hope as defined by the world is wishy-washy, anxiety-filled, or *luck*.

But *the 'hope' of the Bible is confident, assured expectation*, the certainty that the promises of God, in His written Word, are true and *truth*. Hope is not seen but believed. Hope is always *future*; it is the foundation ground of faith.

Faith is defined in Scripture as being "the substance (reality) of things hoped for, the evidence (proof) of things not seen" (Heb. 1:1). *Faith is where hope (assured belief) is combined with action, where we see and act on those unseen things as real.* Perhaps we could show this as a formula: (faith = hope + action). Without faith, the gifts will be inoperative in our lives. It is faith that allows us to operate the gifts in the *now*, and hope, which allows us *to see*, in part, *the future as God sees it*.

Classifying the Gifts

So that we can see the purpose and the effect of the various gifts on our lives, and on the lives of others, we have classified each gifting by what they do:

Revelatory gifts: those gifts that reveal a part of what God sees or knows. These would include the word of wisdom, word of knowledge, discerning of spirits, and teaching.

Speaking gifts: those gifts that use our speech to say something God is saying. This would include faith, tongues, interpretation of tongues, prophecy, and exhortation.

Power gifts: those gifts that give evidence of God's supernatural power to act on His creation. (These gifts are activated by prayer and the work of faith.) The gifts include the working of miracles, healings, giving, service, mercy, leadership, and the laying on of hands.

The Prompting by the Holy Spirit

With your baptism in the Holy Spirit, you received your initial prompting through one of two "signs." The first is "speaking in an unknown tongue," yet many do not respond to this sign because their theology or denominational restrictions *quench their faith* to receive this prompting, (1 Thess. 5:19,20). The second sign is to *preach the word with boldness*, which is also called *prophesying* (Acts 4:31). You may not have ever considered yourself a "preacher," but the infilling of the Holy Spirit *will propel you strongly and urgently to tell someone about Jesus.*

As your gift begins to sprout, *remember, just as your gifts are given to you by the Holy Spirit, they are distributed to us as He (the Holy Spirit) wills; not as you will* (1 Cor. 12:11). The activation and display of these gifts are a collaboration of God's prompting and you acting in faith to carry out what He has gifted you to do.

The unction, (which is like a pressing or pushing in your inward being) will motivate you to attempt to walk in the gifts you have been given. Usually at least one is revealed right away; others may be revealed over time. Once you have received your gift, they can be stirred up—fanned into flame—by worshipping (including using music, singing, "psalms, hymns, and spiritual songs" to the Lord), fasting, fervent prayer, reading the Scripture, and praying in tongues (2 Kings 3:15; Acts 13:2, 3; Col. 3:15; Eph. 5:18–20). *But it is still the Holy Spirit who provides the timing for their activation.* With the approval of your overseers, after being prompted, step out in faith, and be used of God.

The
Revelation
Gifts

CHAPTER FIVE

THE REVELATION GIFTS

—————— ❄ ——————

The revelation gifts reveal a part of what God sees or knows: word of wisdom, word of knowledge, discernment of spirits, and the teaching gift.

The Word of Wisdom

Since the writing of the New Testament, the word of wisdom has been defined in many ways. Some have said that it is "wisdom given to us by God when we ask him." (See James 1:5.) This type of wisdom—let us call it biblical wisdom—is available to all Christians, enabling them to make godly decisions on a regular basis. This biblical wisdom can be obtained through prayer, diligent study, comprehension, and obedience in following scriptural advice. Therefore, it could not be a specific gift of the Holy Spirit because it is available for every born-again believer. Additionally, the word of wisdom is different from biblical wisdom in that *biblical wisdom requires work*. In the word of wisdom, the Holy Spirit does the work; *we receive*.

Some have renamed the 'word of wisdom' as the "gift of wisdom," which it *is not*. King Solomon (1 Kings 3:12; Eccles. 1:13) was given the "gift of wisdom" where he investigated all things under the sun. But the 'word of wisdom' does not give wisdom in everything; no, only a small part. It is a small portion of God's *foreknowledge* concerning a specific situation or circumstance.

So, What Is the *Word of Wisdom*?

The 'word of wisdom' is the supernatural revealing to the understanding in a believer of a part of God's plans and will for a person, or even a place or thing, *in the future*. The word of wisdom reveals God's hope, therefore "it is always speaking to the future" (*The Holy Spirit and His Gifts,* p.71; Luke 21:14, 15; Eph. 5:17). The Scripture reads:

> That the God of our Lord Jesus Christ, the Father of glory, may give to you, the spirit of wisdom and revelation in the knowledge of Him, the eyes of your understanding being enlightened; that you may know what is the *hope* of His calling... (Eph. 1:17–18).

This quote from Ephesians both highlights and affirms what the word of wisdom is to do.

As in all the revelation gifts the 'word of wisdom' is not something you have to work at to obtain. It is dropped into your human spirit, enabling you to become aware of God's plan, purpose, or will, in the future for your own life or of another's life. The revelation of this gifting, like all the gifts, is *only in part*. This is only a word of wisdom, a fragmentary part of God's plan, purpose, and hope for the saints.

Personal note: when the word of wisdom first began in my life, it started in a series of dreams. As the Holy Spirit stepped in, it seemed as if I was having a conversation with God. I began to ask him, "What do these things in the dream mean?" And He responded to me by making clear the meaning of the symbols shown to me in the dream. These revelations were given to me to show me how the enemy was going to attempt to attack my wife and family soon, and what I needed to do to protect them from these attacks—I was to pray.

How Can You Know If This Gift Operates in Your Life?

The 'word of wisdom' can be birthed in dreams while sleeping, where God reveals his plans and purposes to you. Or it can appear in visions where you are awake, but your mind drifts into a deep meditative state, allowing God to speak to you, His will. (See Acts 9:15; 16:9; 18:9, 10).

The 'word of wisdom' may be heard by the gifted believer as an audible voice (see Acts 8:29; 9:4–7). It can be manifested in your human spirit (See Acts 11:28, 13:11). The word of wisdom gives hope, direction, and assurance in difficult times. (Acts 27:23). The 'word of wisdom' can provide instructions and steps to take, *laying the groundwork to establish the necessary faith* that activates the power gifts in our lives (such as healings, working of miracles, service, etc., (Isa. 38:4–8. The 'word of wisdom' is *the spiritual gift that operated in the Old Testament prophets* allowing them to see and speak *the future*. Many people call it prophesying, but in the New Testament, to prophesy has a *different meaning* as we shall see.

The 'word of wisdom' can also be conditional, especially if it is to warn people of a coming judgment or a chastening in their life. A believer's response can change the circumstance, causing the future to change in God's plans, will, and purpose. A 'word of wisdom' was delivered to King Hezekiah by the prophet Isaiah saying, "set thine house in order, for thou shalt die and not live" (see 2 Kings 20:1–6 KJV). Hezekiah's prayer held back the judgment of God on his death, added fifteen years to his life, and held back the judgment for the entire nation into the future. Isaiah received a second 'word of wisdom', showing that with Hezekiah's repentance, the circumstances had changed, and now through the 'word of wisdom', he would be directed in how to receive healing.

A second example is Jonah who was given a 'word of wisdom' for the coming destruction of the city of Nineveh in forty days, yet with the city's repentance, their judgment was removed to a future date (Jonah 1:2; 3:10; 4:2, Nahum 3:1).

Activating the Gift

If you sense that God has given you the gift of the 'word of wisdom', review the above Scripture references. Pray that the Holy Spirit will show *you* how the gift has operated in the past in your life. Share your corresponding experiences with your church overseers. Have them pray with you and for you, seeing if they sense and agree that this is one of God's giftings in your life. When prompted by the Holy Spirit, share with your church authorities by saying, "I believe the Lord has revealed …," *and if they agree*, share your 'word of wisdom' for the saints.

The Word of Knowledge

This refers to the supernatural revelation by the Holy Spirit that gives the believer to know *in part* what God knows concerning a person, place, or thing. This knowledge is needful in that it often reveals what God knows of the spiritual condition in the inner man. The 'word of knowledge' *speaks to things in the present or clarifies things in the past*. The 'word of knowledge' is extremely needful in witnessing to others about Jesus. For the Lord to reveal through the 'word of knowledge' someone's true spiritual condition can be life changing. Jesus operated in the 'word of knowledge' as He witnessed to the woman at the well (see John 4:18, 19).

Personal Note: Even in our personal experience, we have seen the 'word of knowledge' result in fruit for God. Our church outreaches to our community through an idea we got from the believers in Texas that they called the "prayer stop." We have modified it and call it, "the prayer stand." We give out snacks, water, and prayer to passersby on the main streets of our city. Seeing our sign, two men stopped and begin to share with us their excitement about their church's new building, its growth, and its ministry to the community. They were "trustees" for their church, and we rejoiced with them at their success. As they began to leave, the Holy Spirit dropped into us a 'word of knowledge' that we must witness to them about their need to receive the Lord Jesus as their Savior. So, we asked them, "If you died today do you know for sure that you would be with the Lord?" Their reply stunned us, as they said, "I didn't know that anyone could know that for sure." Well, we assured them and showed them from the Scriptures that they could and prayed with them to receive God's grace through faith in Jesus Christ. That day, two men who had been depending on their works to get into heaven learned how to believe the promises of God by faith. God gave us a 'word of knowledge' on these men's spiritual condition leading to their salvation. (Praise the Lord forever!)

What the Word of Knowledge *Is Not*

It is not the gift of knowledge! The knowledge that is obtained through the 'word of knowledge' is not gained by study or research. "It is not natural knowledge or mother wit. It is not photographic memory, scholarly knowledge or even having an encyclopedic knowledge of the Scripture" (The Holy Spirit and His Gifts, pp. 77–88).

Some examples from the Scriptures showing the 'word of knowledge' in action are Acts 8:23—Peter exposing Simon the sorcerer's true motives; Acts 16:6, 7, 9—Paul's travel instructions; and the glorified Jesus's words about the churches to John, in Revelation, chapters 2 and 3.

The 'word of knowledge', and the 'word of wisdom' can sometimes work together. In Acts 9:10–12, Ananias, a believer in ancient Damascus, receives the 'word of knowledge' in a vision revealing Saul's present and past spiritual condition. And then in Acts 9:15–16, we see the 'word of wisdom', revealing God's plans for Saul's future.

What Happens When the Word of Knowledge Is in Operation?

The 'word of knowledge' can be given through dreams and visions (Acts 10:10–16). It can be revealed through the human spirit (Acts 10:19, 20; 13:9–11). The 'word of knowledge' reveals the secret of the hearts of unbelievers. It can lead an unbeliever to conviction of their sin and cause them to acknowledge that God is truly in us (1 Cor. 14:24).

An important word of Advice:

God does not give His gift so that you can think you know other people's business in general or become a gossip, busybody, or a slanderer. No gift of God should result in sinful motives or actions on the gifted believer's part. The word of knowledge is not something you have to work up or guess at. You do not have to examine someone's eyes, clothing, or tendencies to figure out what to say. You are not trying to "read" people. *Those who attempt to do these things are walking after their flesh and not the Spirit.* God gives enough of His 'word of knowledge' to make the hearer know for sure, that God is speaking to them through you. Say only what God give you and leave it at that.

Has the 'word of knowledge' been a gift you have been given?

Pray asking God for clarity and assurance in His direction. Share with your spiritual overseers what you believe God has revealed by His 'word of knowledge' to you. Pray with your fellow saints and your overseers that God will manifest clearly to them that the 'gift' is operating in you. By two or three witnesses, let God 'gift' be established in you.

The Discerning of spirits

The gift of Discerning of spirits is where the Holy Spirit allows the believer to perceive things or 'beings' that are in the spirit realm. This gift also allows the believer not only to perceive the evil, but to see the good, "Discerning of spirits may be discerning the similitude of God, the seraphim, archangels, the 'hosts' of heaven or Satan and his legions. Also, the discerning of the human spirit, the good or the evil tendencies of the spirit or the power that is evil or good that may be behind any manifestation. "(The Holy Spirit and His Gifts, pg. 77-88)".

You might ask, what is the spirit realm?

It is the invisible dimension, (invisible to us) around our earth that the Scripture calls, 'chains of darkness', (2 Peter 2:4). God has made it a 'spiritual prison for the rebellious angels those who refuse to accept the elevation of humans over them. (Genesis 1:26-28). According to the Scriptures one-third of the created angel population joined in this rebellion lead by an 'cherub' class angel named 'Lucifer'- better known today as 'Satan' or 'the devil'. (Rev. 12:4, Isa. 14:12-14, Eze.28:12-15).

Though prevented from physical contact because of the dimensional prison, he found out that he could communicate to humans by implanting 'thoughts' in their minds. He successfully deceived the first couple, (Adam and Eve) Resulting in a corruption and separation of the human spirit from God, mental rebellion, and physical destruction leading to death. It looked as if he has won, until Jesus Christ died and rose from the dead, installing the gospel that would overcome his lies.

Satan's main goal is to keep people away from the gospel of Jesus Christ. The gospel has the power to enliven the human spirit, renew the mind and soul, and to bring awareness to the believer of their new spiritual identity, that gives them authority over the devil, gifts of the spirit, and most importantly ETERNAL LIFE. Despite all this, Satan, uses deceit, lies, fear, to try to keep people comfortable in their 'sinful nature' rejecting God through following and serving him.

The Christian needs the gift of 'Discerning of Spirit to identify the spiritual things of God, from the deceptions of the devil.

What the Discerning of Spirit is NOT!

> *"It is not spiritual though reading nor psychological insight, nor mental penetration. It is not power to discern faults in others nor discerning the character of people, but spirits that operate in and around people." (The Holy Spirit and His Gifts)*

God wants us to be aware of Satan's deceptive nature and his hidden two-pronged agenda: for us to worship Satan like God, (Isa. 14:14) and his hidden plan to keep us in servitude to him.

The body of Christ is called to "have no fellowship with the unfruitful works of darkness, but rather expose them...but all things that are exposed are made manifest by the light" (Eph. 5:11, 13). The gift of discernment of spirits enables us to see the satanic influences behind the scenes of darkness and expose them.

In these end times, that have progressed to 'the great falling away', (2 Thess. 2:3) people will be listening to and accepting the thoughts that are broadcast to all of us by "deceiving spirits and doctrines of devils" (1 Tim. 4:1 KJV). These false doctrines are very persuasive and deceptive by painting the evil as good and the good as evil. Among some of these heresies and deceptions in our present day are the theory of evolution, (which is not science but a philosophical "religion"), post-modernism. (a.k.a. deconstruction); political correctness; sexual perversion; spiritualism; and gender confusion, among others.

From ancient times some spirits of the past are still operating today under new names; such as the worship of the Abominations of Molech, and Milcom (now known as Abortion, and infanticide) occult groups promoting seances, consulting the dead, seeking the words of mediums, witches, warlocks, tarot cards, psychics (California or otherwise), medicine men, candle burning or witch doctors, and all false religions that reject the Lordship of Jesus.

What about "Aliens"?

Demonic deception is behind the popular belief and acceptance of aliens, alien communication, and abduction. Satan's goal is for people to believe that aliens are the superior beings (gods) from another planet that seeded evolution and then influenced the ignorant brutish ape men—archaic humans—to develop the marvelous civilizations of ancient times. Unfortunately, this deception has convinced the producers of the History Channel to suggest to their viewers that the idea of aliens from outer space is 'true' history. What is closer to the truth is that the aliens are from *inner space* (fallen angels) under chains of darkness who by deception, deceit, cunning, and psychological manipulation, including hypnosis is corrupting the thinking of many today. (See Genesis 3:1–4; Isa. 14:12–15; Ezek. 28:12–17; Eph.2:2; 1 Pet. 2:1, 4.)

Again, the gift of 'discernment of spirits' *is revelation*, and it does not involve any work (no candles, fires, not even "fasting," etc.) on the believer's part. God makes you aware of the spiritual realm. The Scripture warns us, "Little children, keep yourselves from idols, amen" (1 John 5:21).

We can see this gift in operation where the Holy Spirit reveals to Peter the satanic source as Ananias and his wife, try to deceive God and the church of God, to gain vain glory. "But Peter said, "Ananias, why has Satan filled your heart to lie to the Holy Spirit?"" (Acts 5:3).

In Acts 13:9, 10 the Apostle Paul also is used of God in 'discerning of spirits' that were operating in a man named Elymas Bar Jesus. He was a Jewish sorcerer and false prophet who attempted to resist Paul and Barnabas as they shared the gospel with a Roman official, (a Proconsul), "Then Saul, who *is called* Paul, filled with the Holy Ghost, set his eyes on him and said, "O full of all subtlety and all mischief, thou child of the devil, *thou* enemy of all righteousness, will thou not cease to pervert the right ways of the Lord?" (KJV).

There is one important principal for those with this gift of discerning of spirits: the Holy Spirit will protect you in the operation of this gift, in seeing or sensing the spirit realm, *but be very careful not to attempt to work up or stir up this gift*. Spirts are very deceptive, so do not seek them. This is a revelation gift, given to the believer as the Holy Spirit wills, not as you will. The Scriptures warns us to *test the spirits*.

Does This Gift Operate in You?

Study the Scriptures, (see the examples above). Pray for guidance by the Holy Spirit. Share what you believe you have sensed, felt, or saw spiritually with your church overseers so that they might pray with you and over you and to see if they witness that this gifting is in you. If so, let them lay hands on you, praying for the continued manifestation of this gift in your life. Under their oversight, move out in faith and share what you believe the Holy Spirit has revealed to you.

The Teaching Gift

The gift of teaching is where the Holy Spirit imparts His revelation and insight, allowing the holy Scriptures to be understood and applied with God's intent and meaning. The teaching gift affects the hearers by *reorienting the mind of the Christian to the obedience of Christ*. The teaching gift results in exposing and refuting wrong doctrines and motives and increases faith in Jesus (see 1 Tim. 2:7; Acts 17:1–3; 18:24–27; Titus 1:7–9; Ps. 51:12–13).

The teaching gift is evident when the Holy Spirit opens the Scriptures, immersing the teacher in greater understanding and knowledge of Jesus and enabling him/her to share this with other Christians. The teaching gift is not just knowing the Scriptures or even to expound them eloquently. Individuals can be trained and taught in schools (Christian or secular) to teach others on many topics, but the spiritual gift of teaching infuses God's Scriptures with new life and different perspectives that only God could reveal, thereby bringing joy to the teacher and enlightenment to the hearer who in turn can enlighten others.

Let us look at the biblical example of Apollos, as described to us in Acts 18, "now a certain Jew named Apollos, born at Alexandria, an eloquent man, and mighty in the Scriptures came to Ephesus. This man had been instructed in the way of the Lord, and being fervent in spirit, he spoke and taught accurately the things of the Lord, though he knew only the baptism of John" (Acts 18:24–26).

This man had attended the best schools of his day, he was a Jew giving him entry in the synagogues, and he had memorized, internalized, and shared with others the truths of God's Word—even undoubtedly that Jesus was the Messiah, "so, he began to speak boldly in the synagogue. When Aquila and Priscilla heard him, they took him aside, and explained to him the way of God more accurately."

Please note: the spirit-filled Christians listening to his teaching noted something was missing. He was saying the right things, fervently, boldly, but empowered by his human spirit and not the Holy Spirit. What did Aquilla and Priscilla explain to him? I believe it was his need for the baptism in the Holy Spirit. The experience of Pentecost was obviously something he was not aware. Why do I say this? In Acts 19:1–7, the apostle Paul meets twelve Jewish men who are called disciples. They had been taught and believed that Jesus was the Messiah, and it is possible they had been taught this by or with Apollos. Yet Paul also, like Aquilla and Priscilla, noted something was missing. Paul instructs them to be water baptized in the name of the Lord Jesus, "and when Paul had laid hands on them, the Holy Spirit came upon them, and they spoke with tongues and prophesied" (Acts 19:6).

We may be as Apollos, trained, educated, and inspired to teach the Word. But without the teaching gift coming from your baptism in the Holy Spirit, your teaching will lack the convicting, clarifying, enlightening power that reorients the thinking from dependence on the world to total dedication to Jesus (see John 3:2).

Do You Have the Teaching Gift?

To teach is a natural process of life. Parents teach their children. Spouses teach each other in marriages, employers teach and train employees, teachers teach students, and on and on. The ministry gift of 'teaching' mentioned in 1 Corinthians 12:28 and Ephesians 4:12 *requires Holy Spirit–gifted individuals to fill these ministries.* Many think that training in school in theology, doctrine, and worldview automatically can make one a Holy Spirit–gifted teacher. Not so, the teaching gift is a gifting that must be waited on (Rom. 12:6), with *waited on* meaning, "to be developed and tested, to see if it is genuine."

The spiritual gift of teaching is evidenced as the reader of the Bible gains a revelation of God's purpose and intent by "comparing spiritual things (the holy Scriptures) with spiritual things (Holy Spirit revelation)" (1 Cor.2:13; Heb. 5:14). The teaching gift allows the gifted believer to see new insights in Scriptures that he/she may have read many times before (see Heb. 5:14) and enables the teacher to live as he teaches (see Rom. 2:21–24; Titus 2:3; 1 Pet. 3:15–16). The gift of teaching enables the Believer to see God's revelation of Himself in nature, and all His creation (see 1 Cor. 11:14; Rom. 1:19–22). It also refutes and exposes false doctrine (see 2 Tim. 4:2–4; Acts 18:28). The gift of teaching can (and in many cases does) lead to the ministry of teaching (see 1 Cor. 12:28; Eph. 4:11). Be aware that this will catapult you into a great deal of personal responsibility as to what you speak. "My brothers, let not many of you become teachers, knowing that we shall receive stricter judgment" (James 3:1). But rejoice, those who overcome will reap greater rewards.

Do you think God is developing this gift in you? Contact your church leaders; tell them what you feel is your gifting. Let them pray with you and over you. Read the Scriptures line by line and write down your insights (Isa. 28:10). The Lord will teach you and make room for you to practice your gifting.

The "Speaking" Gifts

CHAPTER SIX

THE SPEAKING GIFTS

These gifts use our speech to say something God is saying. This grouping includes faith, different kinds of tongues, Interpretation of tongues, prophecy, and exhortation.

The Gift of Faith

The term *faith* can have many meanings in the Bible and in our daily lives. The Scriptures reveal that there are at least four types of faiths: *natural faith*, which everyone is born with to some degree; *saving faith*, which settles in when we respond to the conviction of the Holy Spirit that we are sinners and declare Christ as our Lord and Savior; *biblical faith*, which acts on the revelations of the Word of God; and the *spiritual gift of faith*, which we will call *God's faith* to separate it from the others.

Natural Faith: Everybody has been given faith but not the same amount of faith (Rom. 12:3). Natural faith is intrinsic to humanity. It is what enables humans to believe something and act on that belief. This faith, supplied by God, is made available through our ability to reason (See Isa. 1:18, Rom. 1:19, 20) and causes us to believe and act on those things that *we think are true*, or that we see as reality.

Just about all things that are accomplished by humans start with this natural faith. It is what motivates us to accomplish what we have believed in our hearts. Through natural faith, discoveries are made, and inventions, buildings, and lifestyles are constructed (Gen. 4:18–22). One biblical example of this faith in operation is the faith confession of the people at the building of the Tower of Babel (Gen. 11:3–6). What is most revealing in this portion of Scripture is God's response to the power of human faith, "now nothing that they propose to do will be withheld from them." These humans had faith in their own human power and not in God. This thing was so powerful that only God could stop them from unifying their different measures of faith and accomplishing a disobedient and untimely outcome.

But because of God's grace, when through natural faith we believe God's truth, then our natural faith facilitates a 'saving faith'.

Saving faith: This occurs when natural faith responds to the gospel, as we understand and choose to believe and receive the grace offered by the blood of Jesus Christ, "by grace you are saved through faith, it is the gift of God, so that no man can boast" (Eph. 2:8, 9).

Biblical faith: After salvation, your faith increases and matures through fellowship with other Christians (1 John 1:7), reading, learning, hearing, and obeying the Scriptures and responding to the voice of the Holy Spirit in your everyday life decisions. (See Rom. 10:17). You become steadfast and assured in believing the truth of the Bible. Biblical faith encourages us to experiment with the parameters of speaking back to God the promises that He has made us. And then, through the power of the Holy Spirit, *we declare, and act on what God has said*. We find that we can obtain the things (physically and spiritually) that He has provided for us in this age. The sure byproduct of biblical faith is obedience (Matt. 7:7, 8; 21:22; John 16:24).

The gift of faith, or God's faith, operates within the parameters of the will of God and the Word of God. It is a supernatural manifestation given by the Holy Spirit, allowing a believer to *speak a word, without doubt,* and *receive a miraculous result.* This gift operates in such a way that *God honors the believer's words as His own* and miraculously brings those words to pass.

Examples of the gift of faith operating are found in 1 Kings 17:1 (Elijah, "no dew or rain but according to my word), Matthew 8:23–27 (Jesus calms the sea), Acts 4:29–30 (disciples' prayer), *and the Scripture that defines the gift*: Matthew 21, that says, "So Jesus answered and said to them, "Assuredly I say to you, if you have faith and do not doubt, you will not only do what was done to the fig tree, but also if you say to this mountain, "Be removed and be cast into the sea" it will be done. And whatever things you ask in prayer, believing, you will receive" (Matt. 21:21, 22).

What makes this faith unique and different from all other faiths is *no work is required*, at least no work from the believer's part. All other faiths require some work or action that responds to the words of faith that are spoken; however, since God honors this faith as His own faith, He is the one doing the action and we receive what He is doing. *"The gift of faith is a gift of the Spirit, to the believer, that he might receive miracles"* (*The Holy Spirit and His Gifts,* p. 84).

Since the gift of faith, being a portion of God's faith, (Rom. 3:3; Mark 11:22) requires no work or action from the believer, the anointed believer speaks the words that are the desire of God (Mark 11:22, 23; 2 Cor. 4:13; Acts 9:37–43; 27:22–25) those words will receive a miracle.

The Gift of Faith in Operation

In the Bible, the gift of faith is involved in raising the dead (Acts 9:40–41), healing of long-term illnesses (Acts 9:33–35), the work of angels (Acts

27:22–25) and *seeing* faith in others that can produce miracles in that person's life (Acts 14:9–10).

Have you been given the gift of faith? It is a gift that you can ask for. The Holy Spirit gives the gift of faith as He wills. Although we each are given an initial gift, I believe the Holy Spirit can and will bless us with *temporary manifestations of any gifting for those doing the will of God.* Having suggested that, I think a Christian should expect the gift of faith to operate, especially as we evangelize in these end times. We can pray, as the saints of Acts 4:29 did, for the gift of faith, that it might become actualized among our congregations so that unbelievers will become astonished by the power of God. God is willing to increase our faith to the point that we do not doubt. If you are spirit-filled, you may receive it.

Develop your faith walk with biblical faith and you may grow into it.

The Gift of Tongues: The Sign, the Prayer, the Prophecy

Biblically speaking, *the spiritual gift of speaking in unknown tongues can be a 'sign'. It has also been given to aid our personal prayer life, enabling us to pray IN the Spirit.* A tongue spoken aloud during a service is a prophetic word that *must be interpreted* so that all the congregation can hear the interpretation, judge it, and "hold fast that which is good" (1 Thess. 5:19). In this section, we will look at it as a sign and as an enabling activity designed by God so we may worship and pray in the Spirit. The interpretation of tongues is a separate gift.

Tongues as a Sign:

In Acts 2:33, it was a *'sign' to the believing disciples of the first century* that the Holy Spirit had been sent by Jesus. It was the *'sign' given by God for every generation,* allowing believers to know when God had fulfilled his promise of filling them individually with the Holy Spirit (Please read Acts 2:38–39). It was the 'sign' to believing Jews that believing Gentiles were also in Christ and fellow members in the Body of Christ, (not by diet, Sabbath, clothing, or circumcision but by being filled with the Holy Spirit), Acts 10:45. It remains a 'sign' of the Baptism in the Holy Spirit today.

But it is more than a 'sign'. It is a spiritual gift, enabling each Christian *to pray and worship in spirit and in truth*. It provides the "spiritual sacrifices" (1 Pet. 2:5) needed to fulfil our role as "priest" to our High Priest, Jesus Christ (see John 4:23, Heb. 3:1, 1 Peter 2:5,9, 1 Cor. 14:14.).

It is the gift that enables *personal edification*. (1 Cor. 14:2, 4).

What Is Personal Spiritual Edification?

The defilement of the human spirit, (heart) was impossible to "clean" under the Old Covenant. No matter how hard one my try we are unable to keep the whole Law, "for whoever shall keep the whole law and yet stumble in one point, he is guilty of all", (James 2:10; Gal. 3:10). Our acceptance of Jesus Christ, and the blood of His sacrifice forged a *New Covenant* for us. *Before* our receiving Jesus's inward presence, our spiritual heart's condition was "deceitful above all *things* and desperately wicked; who can know it?" (Jer. 17:9 KJV). And it was *impossible* to clean our "hearts" as Proverbs 20: 9 says, "Who can say, 'I have made my heart clean; I am pure from my sin?" (KJV)

At our salvation God did what no human can do; *He cleaned our hearts* (1 Pet. 1:22, Heb. 10:22). *Hallelujah!* But through the baptism in the Holy Spirit, He has provided a way to "build on" and maintain that cleansing through personal edification *that the Holy Spirit now enables us to do by praying in the Spirit, - "speaking in tongues"* - as the Spirit gives us utterance.

For he that speaketh in an unknown tongue speaketh *not* unto men *but unto God* for no man understands him. Howbeit in the spirit he speaketh mysteries... He that speaketh in an unknown tongue *edifies himself... (1 Cor. 14:2,4)*

Speaking in tongues enables us to *worship* in spirit and truth.

In the gospel of John, the Lord Jesus was directed by the Holy Spirit to travel through Samaria. As His disciples left Him to buy food, He met a woman drawing water at the well. He asks for her to draw Him some water for a drink. Through a short conversation He reveals to her that He is a savior, a prophet, and as a man so connected to God, that *He knows how the Father wants and requires to be worshipped by humans,* He says:

The hour cometh and now is, when the true worshippers shall worship the Father in spirit and truth; for the Father seeketh such to worship Him. God is a Spirit and they that worship Him *must* worship Him in Spirit and in truth. (John 4:23, 24 KJV)

Could the apostle Paul be showing us that prayer by "speaking in other tongues is a *must* worship for born-again believers?

For if I pray in an unknown tongue *my spirit prayeth*, but my understanding is unfruitful. What is it then? I will pray *with the spirit* and will pray with the understanding (1 Cor. 14:2, 4, 14, 15 KJV).

> *It appears that praying in the spirit and praying in tongues are the same. It enables us to worship and give back to God what He loves.*

The apostle Paul wished that all believers (in Corinth and those that were to read the epistle) spoke in tongues (1 Cor. 14:5), and he even noted that he spoke in tongues himself more than them all (1 Cor. 14:18). Why do you suppose the apostle would encourage that for the body of Christ? *I propose that it is to give God control of our "tongue problem."*

> But the tongue, can no man tame, it is an unruly evil full of deadly poison... Out of the same mouth proceedeth blessing and cursing. My brethren these things ought not so to be. (James 3:8, 10 KJV)

James assures us that *no man* can control the tongue. *But God* has given us His way that He can control our words to Him and supply the spiritual ability to control our speech to our fellow man. Praying in the spirit is *pure* prayer, allowing His words to speak through us, true spiritual worship and establishes a way that we can "clean" our hearts so we might control our speech enabling us to speak words of grace to our fellow man. It is God's way to tame the tongue (James 3:6–8).

To speak in an unknown tongue requires faith in the Holy Scriptures that reveal to us it is God's will and blessing for us. And faith to believe that God has chosen this way to signal to us that we have received His promise and presence in our lives. It also takes the assurance to know that praying and worshipping in tongues is pleasing to God, and He desires and enables those to worship him in this way (John 4:23, 1 Cor. 14:2). It requires the action of faith to yield our mouths to move, our breath to exhale, and our tongues to articulate words that we do not understand yet know that we are speaking mysteries of worship and prayers directly to God. Yielding our tongue to God to worship and pray affects our whole body. When God has our tongue, He has our whole being. Yielding to the Holy Spirit by speaking in tongues is to walk in God's ways and begins our life of victory allowing our faith to overcome our flesh.

Tongues are primarily for personal spiritual edification, spiritual worship to God, and our first step to "stifle" the "sinful nature" to the obedience of Christ (see 1 Cor. 14:28).

Important Points of Order

Holy Spirit–gifted tongues and prophesy are not uncontrollable ecstatic utterances forced upon the speaker by controlling spirits. The spiritual gift of tongues, interpretation of tongues, and prophecy are *the result of cooperation* as the Holy Spirit imparts and prompts the gift in you, and then you, by faith, move (or speak in this case), expecting and receiving the spiritual results.

Timing: As with all the speaking gifts, *the gift does not control you; you control the gift.* The Scripture speaks to this in saying, "and the spirits of the prophets are subject to the prophets" (1 Cor. 14:32). You can hold what the Holy Spirit has prompted you until the right time or order in the service (See 1 Cor. 14:26–32).

Personal note: I believe that all saints have available to them three gifts: tongues, prophecy, and exhortation. These three gifts of the Holy Spirit are expressed in the Scriptures to be for all saints: tongues for edification and worship; exhortation enabling one saint to edify and build up another saint; and prophecy for the comfort, direction, warning, and encouragement of the local church. But all spiritual gifts of God must be received and acted on by faith.

Do you have the gift of tongues? If you are in Christ and baptized in His Spirit, *you already have the gift of tongues*. The real question is, have you allowed your faith to access this gift that is in you? Pray for this evidence of His infilling. Expect God to fill your mouth with His words, even though you will not understand them. Open your mouth in worship, praise, and adoration of God in your native tongue, and when you run out, God will fill you with His words, which in your natural ability you could not utter.

Praise God!

The Gift of Interpretation of Tongues

Any church where the speaking of tongues is allowed *as a public spoken word* must have someone with this gift. To have this gift operating in you, you should be someone who has received the expression of the gift of tongues. The gift of interpretation is a tandem gift, meaning it does not work alone. The Holy Spirit must first prompt the believer who speaks in tongues to know (and be assured in his spirit) that the public utterance in tongues is a word for the entire congregation, (1 Cor.14:27.28). Then, after hearing this utterance, those who are aware of the gifts operating in their lives are to pray for the interpretation (1 Cor. 14:12, 13, 17). The purpose of interpretation of the tongue spoken is so that the entire church will be edified by understanding God's will for the church. The interpretation will be a prophetic word, speaking edification, exhortation, and comfort to the church.

Do you have the gift of interpreting of tongues? After praying for God to use you in interpretation, wait until you have received the first word in your native tongue from the Holy Spirit. Then speak out, as God will give you the rest as you step out in faith.

The interpretation of tongues is *not a word-for-word translation* of what was spoken in tongues, but it is an *interpretation*. A long word spoken in tongues may be interpreted into our tongue in a much shorter time. In addition, several saints may interpret different segments of the same word spoken in tongues to complete the full interpretation (1 Cor. 14:31). The gift of interpretation of tongues is for the gathered body of Christ, and not usually for an individual, and will never condemn the people of God.

The interpretation of tongues is one form of New Testament prophecy, It must therefore be judged (evaluated by sensing spiritual agreement of the interpretation) by *our spirit*, the *holy Scriptures*, and *church* elders, leaders, and overseers.

The Gift of Prophecy

"Therefore brethren, desire earnestly to prophesy" (1 Cor. 14:39).

The gift of prophecy is words spoken under the unction, the prompting, of the Holy Spirit *in your native language*, that edify (builds up), exhort (counsel, warns), and comfort those to whom you are speaking (1 Cor. 14:3; Rom. 14:19; 15:2, 4, 5).

At this point let me remind you that there is a difference in the spiritual 'gift of prophecy' given though the Holy Spirit (1 Cor. 12:9) and the 'ministry of prophecy', which is ordered by Jesus (Eph. 4:11). The 'ministry' may include several of the spiritual gifts operating at the same time (word of wisdom, word of knowledge, discerning of spirits, working of miracles, gifts of healings, etc.) But the gift of prophecy given by the Holy Spirit to individuals is a bit simpler. The Holy Spirit's gift of prophecy primarily speaks to individuals in the church in three areas: edification, exhortation, and comfort (1 Cor. 14:3).

When the gift of prophecy is spoken to a believer it will result in edification—being built up as we learn God's direction for our life; exhortation—which includes encouragement and warning, giving clear directions as supplied by the Holy Spirit; and comfort—in knowing that God knows us personally and is with us.

The gift of prophecy *also affects unbelievers*. Prophecy is a 'sign' to unbelievers convincing and convicting them. The prophetic words will expose the secrets of their hearts, leading some to worship God and some to testify that God is truly in us and with us (1 Cor. 14:24, 25; 2 Kings 5:10,15; Jonah 1:10–16).

Judging Prophecy

The spiritual gift of prophecy is to be spoken to individuals in the church setting so that some of the leadership, or mature saints can hear it and discern it to be of God. The believer to whom the prophecy is spoken should also discern whether it is true in their own spirit. This control allows the saint to whom the prophecy is given, to know whether the source of the prophesy is the speaker's good intentions or by Holy Spirit revelation. As a gifted believer is learning to hear and speak what God is saying, they are also learning to wait and not attempt to use their gift before being prompted by the Holy Spirit.

As we have stated before: the spiritual gift of prophecy is not the ministry of the prophet.

Do you have the gift of prophecy? You probably do because the Scripture says, "for you can all prophesy, one by one" (1 Cor. 14:31). Perhaps these guidelines will help us to operate in this gift.

1. To start in developing the gift of prophecy in our life is to begin to *testify of Jesus Christ* to other saints and to those who will hear you. Testify even when the fear of ridicule or death is in our face because "the testimony of Jesus, is the spirit of prophecy" (Rev. 19:10).

2. We are to covet (desire strongly) to prophesy (1 Cor. 14:39) and pray with expectation of it happening in our lives. Remember God will give us the desire of our hearts (Ps. 37:4; Prov. 16:1–3).

3. Exercise your gift; when you sense a prompting, begin to speak edification, exhortation, and comfort to your fellow believers.

The Holy Spirit will begin to transform your words to His words of prophecy.

The Gift of Exhortation

The gift of exhortation is the supernatural ability given by the Holy Spirit *to speak the word of God with boldness, urgency, and warning; giving spiritual advice that encourages sanctification*—holy living, repentance, and renewal in Christ Jesus. The gift of exhortation operates in two ways. First, on those to whom the words are spoken. The gift causes the hearers to understand, in *their inner man*, that *the words spoken to them have spiritual authority and that they come from God* (Rom. 12:8; Col. 1:27–29; Titus 2:15). Second, through the gift of exhortation, the speaker communicates encouragement, rebuke, or admonishment that results in training in righteousness and correction of doctrinal error (Titus 2:11–15; 2 Tim. 4:2).

The gift is most active in those who preach the gospel, and some prophecy employs the gift of exhortation. This gift, to exhort, can be stirred up in just about all Christians, *especially as we remind each other of the promises and truth of God's Word.* As we are stirred to exhort each other and testify of his transforming power in our lives, we also overcome the devil (Heb. 3:13; Rev. 12, 11). After all, to exhort, (Gk., *paraklesis*) is "to call someone to draw near and walk with God."

What the gift of exhortation *is not*:

- The gift does not give the believer to know other Christians' sins.

- The gift does not speak words of dishonor of other saints (1 Tim. 5) but encourages them to function in God's will for their lives.

- The gift is not to be spoken with self-righteousness or arrogance but with an attitude of love, humility, longsuffering, and teaching (2 Tim. 4:2; Heb. 3:13).

This gift is usually to the gathered church—but it can sometimes be to individuals. The spiritual impact of this gift is that individual believers will sense the authority of the words spoken, be assured that they are from God, and lead them to repentance and sanctification.

Do you have the gift of exhortation? Yes, you probably do! In Hebrews 3:13, Christians are called to exhort each other daily to prevent any of us from allowing sin to deceive us. This gift is set in the body to keep us on guard against the world, the flesh, and the devil. If Christians are directed by the Scripture to exhort each other, it must be a gift available to most Christians.

The two initial signs of being filled with the Holy Spirit were: speaking in an unknown tongue and speaking the Word of God with boldness (Acts 2:40; 4:31; 10:46). The gift of exhortation is synonymous with speaking the Word of God with boldness.

Activating This Gift

As in activating any gift, there are phases of understanding that the Holy Spirit takes us through to grow the gifts in our lives:

1. Identifying the gift and how does it work, and what does it do.

2. Recognizing and accepting it as what God has given you, as a stewardship; and

3. Acting on it in faith to develop it to maturity for the benefit of others.

Signs that the gift of exhortation is ready to work in you:

Have you sensed an urgency to speak to others of God's transformation of your life?

Do you have a deep concern about how some teach grace? Do you want to warn others that grace does not give a right to live an unholy lifestyle, without spiritual consequences? (Gal. 6:7; Rom. 6:22, 23).

Do you feel you are being made ready to give a defense to everyone who asks you a reason for the hope that is in you, with meekness and fear? (1 Pet. 3:15).

Some famous biblical exhorters are John the Baptist (Luke 3:11–19); the apostle Peter (Acts 2:40); the apostle Paul, (1 Thess. 4:1; Titus 1:9); the apostle James (writer of the book of James); and all the "called" of God.

IMPORTANT NOTE: There are many Christian leaders in our day gifted with the gift of exhortation. Many don't believe that all the spiritual gifts are functional in our day and time. But regardless of that the Holy Spirit has STILL given them and us His Sign of His infilling in their lives, THEY ARE PREACHING THE WORD OF GOD WITH BOLDNESS through the 'spiritual gift' of EXHORTATION.

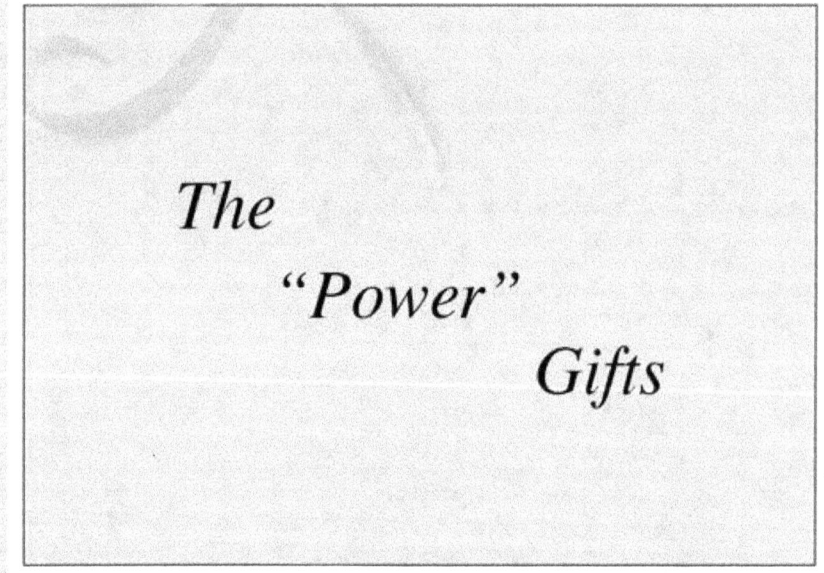

The "Power" Gifts

CHAPTER SEVEN

THE "POWER GIFTS"

The power gifts include the working of miracles, gifts of healings, gifts of giving, gift of leadership, gift of service (aka ministry), gift of mercy, and the laying on of hands.

All the power gifts are activated and fueled by *some type of spiritual faith*: either the gift of faith (aka God's faith) or biblical faith.

The "gift of faith," which we are calling God's faith to differentiate it from biblical faith, is where the Holy Spirit embeds in you *the faith of God*, where you are enabled to speak without doubt and receive a miraculous result. There is *no work or action on your part* to receive this miraculous result. (Please review the chapter discussing the 'faiths'.)

Biblical faith is where you stand trusting in the truth of the Bible as God's written Word, *acting in some manner or way* that you are prompted, assured that through those actions, He will bring about a miraculous result.

The "Power Gifts" as a 'Sign'.

The power gifts are spiritual gifts that are sometimes used as a 'sign' of God's sovereignty to work in the earth in response to the faith of His people. A 'sign' gift can sometimes *operate temporarily in the life of any believer*, especially when God wants to use us to share the gospel or to verify to outsiders that He is truly working in *us*. (Acts 4:29–31; 28:8).

The Gift of Working of Miracles

This gift is in operation as the believer is prompted by the Holy Spirit to do some action (such as touching, holding, laying on of hands, commanding, praying, applying oils, cloths, etc.), resulting in a miraculous outcome. The actual miracle that is done can involve anything God has created. The result can affect persons, the climate, (weather, wind, etc.), the plant and animal kingdoms, inanimate objects, the casting out of demons, and even the raising of the dead. Those prompted by the Holy Spirit, using biblical faith, will receive a miraculous result based on the maturity of their faith. This maturity is not based on the age of the believer, but on the depth of the believer's trust in what God has said. If you are prompted by the Holy Spirit to operate in this gift, He, may be actively stretching your faith. This gift often works in conjunction with the gifts of healings.

Those, who operate in this gift through the gift of faith (which is the faith of God), will speak only what God has prompted them to say and receive a miraculous result.

Examples of this gift in operation are found in Matthew 14:26–27 (Jesus walking on the water), Acts 3:6, 7 (Peter speaking the name of Jesus, and lifting up the man), Acts–8:5–8, 39 (Phillip casting out demons, and later transported from Gaza to Azotus), Acts 14:10 (Paul speaking healing), Acts 19:11 (unusual miracles by the hand of Paul), and Acts 20:9, 10 (the raising the dead).

Do you have the gift of the working of miracles? I am sure that most of us will probably say; no! However, the 'sign' of the working of miracles may have operated in your life. Have you seen miracles as the result of your prayers? Have you been saved from a car, or any accident, as you called on the name of Jesus? I believe one type of working of miracles that all Christians can participate in is the *raising of the dead.* You might ask, how?

Raising the dead is bringing someone from death to life. By sharing the gospel with someone who was dead ("in trespasses and sin" Eph. 2:1), you *are* doing your 'faith action' that raises the dead. Those dead in sin are made alive. When you share the love of Jesus with those who have not received him, you are joining with God as He uses you—through the gift of working of miracles—to lead them to salvation and Eternal Life, (James 5:19,20; Jude 21-23).

I would suggest that you ponder in your heart the true miracles that have happened in your life and investigate if they have been a pattern since your baptism in the Holy Spirit. Ask other Christians and your church leaders to pray with you and see what they say. By two or three witnesses, let every word be established.

The Gifts of Healings

Throughout history, God has desired that his people were to be well, not sick, infirmed, disabled, or diseased. He gave the ancient nation of Israel dietary laws, economic laws, and spiritual laws to limit the effects of 'sin' from destroying them before His fulfillment of bringing the Messiah into the earth. How much more does God desire us to reflect His personal care and protection from the ravages of our world? Though the "wages of 'sin' is death" (Rom. 6:23), by the directions of the Holy Spirit, we can receive life-renewing properties in our mortal bodies to extend our days and to fulfill God's purpose and calling on our lives (Rom. 8:11).

The "gifts of healings," (please notice the plural on this gift), are a combination of spiritual gifts, imparted through the prompting of the Holy

Spirit, and faith, whether biblical faith with work involved; or God's faith with no work involved— only speaking. The result is healing of the body, soul, or spirit of a human, or even the healing of objects on the earth, such as rivers or springs (see 2 Kings 2:21).

These healings are done as the believer *follows precise instructions* by the Holy Spirit, allowing the believer(s) to move in several categories of spiritual gifts (revelatory, speaking, and power giftings).

The revelatory gifts (word of wisdom, word of knowledge, discerning of spirits, etc.) often *reveal* the spiritual source that is behind the actual physical sickness, whether sin and/or the lifestyle it produces (John 5:6) or demonic deception and attack. The speaking gifts (interpretation of tongues, prophecy, exhortation, faith, etc.) are used to council, advise, and direct possible changes in lifestyle (John 5:14; 8:11). And the power gifts (working of miracles, the laying on of hands, the gift of mercy, etc.) add the spiritual muscle to work with the others to impart healings.

Please read these examples of healings resulting from the combination of gifts found in these Scriptures: Acts 9:9–12, 17 (word of wisdom, word of knowledge, laying on of hands); Acts 9:33–34 (word of knowledge and God's faith); in Acts 9:39–41 (prayer of faith, working of miracles, through God's faith); and Acts 28:8, 9 (prayer of faith, working of miracles, laying on of hands).

Faith in Christ's Promises Can Also Produce Healings

"But without faith it is impossible to please Him; for he who cometh to God must believe that He *is*, and that He is a rewarder of them that diligently seek Him" (Heb. 11:6 KJV).

Let us peruse the Scriptures and see where *faith* produces healing results: Matthew 8:5–10, 13 (the centurion believed because he understood how authority works. When Jesus gives the command—speaks the word—it happens, Jesus said it was the centurion great faith in Jesus's authority that produced the result); Matthew 9:22, Mark 5:25–34 (woman with the issue of blood); Mark 9:15–29 (Lord, help my unbelief); Mark 10:47–52 (blind man healed); Luke 17:12–19 (ten lepers walk away believing Jesus command); John 4:47–53 (sick son of the nobleman is healed because the nobleman believes Jesus's word). Be assured as you continue looking on your own, there are many more instances of miracles and healings resulting from believing in and acting in faith on Jesus's word.

Intercessory Prayers: The work of the Church and Individual Believers

James 5:14–16 introduces two additional factors that lead to healings: the prayer of faith, and the effective, fervent prayer of the righteous.

The Prayer of Faith: A work of the Body of Christ, (the Church).

"Is any sick among you? Let him call for the elders of the church, and let them pray over him, anointing him with oil in the name of the Lord" (James 5:14 KJV). *This faith action* signifies the Holy Spirit's sanctifying power, in unity with the church leaders in the name of Jesus (James 5:14 KJV).

Look at the assured results of this type of prayer: "And the prayer of faith, shall save the sick and the Lord shall raise him up. And if he has committed sins, they shall be forgiven" (James 5:15 KJV).

I believe the prayer of faith is asking, petitioning, drawing near to God, through our High Priest Jesus Christ! This 'faith' is propelled by *an assured confidence* by the elders that Jesus has given His Church the right to appear before Christ to obtain mercy and find the grace that God has given through his Church to heal (John 20:23; Mark 16:17–18; Heb.

4:16). The prayer of faith is *spiritual intercession* by the local church for sick members.

The Effective, Fervent Prayer of the Righteous: The work of individual believers toward one another. "Confess *your* faults one to another, and pray one for another, that you may be healed. The effectual, fervent prayer of the *righteous man* availeth much" (James 5:16 KJV).

The effective fervent prayer of the righteous is also intercession, *but mutual intercession, involving the individual saints empathizing with each other through fellowship and love,* praying for one another, exposing their own infirmities and weakness, being assured through God's Word and the Holy Spirit's prompting that their righteousness is from Jesus Christ's sacrifice (1 John 1:6–9). But it starts with repentance of both individuals. *Repentance* and the *fervent heartfelt prayer* for each other results in the faith action that brings healing.

Do you have the gift of healing?

Do you have a strong desire to pray personally for those who are sick?

Do you have prayer partners that you team up with regularly to pray for healing?

Have other Christians prayed for you, and you received healing through the power of the Holy Spirit in response to their prayer?

Have you ever been told that you prayed for a person and God healed them?

Have you ever been prompted by the Holy Spirit to pray for healing?

If you are an elder, minister, or leader in your local church, do you pray the prayer of faith over others? Has anyone reported to you of their healing?

If you believe you have this gift, have your spiritual overseers pray with you. Share with them your experiences. See if they sense the same spiritual gift operating in you. With their permission, and with the prompting of the Holy Spirit, start praying for healing for those in your local congregation. The results will speak for themselves.

A Word of Caution

Since the times of Peter and Paul, people have desired the power to heal, but some have used trickery, deception, and even witchcraft to make us believe *this power rests in them*. (See Acts 8:13–24, Simon the magician.) If Jesus is not credited and glorified, it is not of God. *Be careful of groups that attempt to tie "healings" to your giving to them financially.*

Some have believed that being "healed" by the various gifts of healings, means that you cannot and should not seek medical advice and treatment for physical and some mental conditions. That is not what the Bible teaches. The Psalm reads, "Bless the LORD, O my soul and forget not *all* His benefits, who forgives *all* your iniquities and heals *all* your diseases" (Ps.103:2 KJV). God is to be credited for healing you, regardless of how it comes about. Even Jesus declared in Matt 9:12, those who are well don't need a physician but those who are sick" (KJV). It seems that "healing" comes from God, but *treatment* seems to be the place of the medical community. It is God who has allowed the knowledge, equipment, and techniques to affect treatments that promotes God's healing of the body. In the book of Proverbs, the writer assesses medicine as doing, "good" (Prov. 17:22 KJV). God also directs Isaiah to make a poultice to heal what was killing King Hezekiah (Isa. 38:21). Even the apostle Paul writes a prescription to Timothy to avoid the water and use the wine for his recurring sickness (1 Tim. 5:23). The important thing in receiving healing is that we know that it came from God, even if we get treatment from the medical community.

God continues to make healings available to the church today, but healing on earth is *always temporary*. At the new birth, our spirits are born-again, our souls are renewed by the word of God, and even our bodies may be healed as we change our lifestyles to holy patterns, or we receive God's miraculous touch. However, the sinful nature that is embedded in our natural body through our life blood will cause all of us to physically die eventually (Rom. 8:10; Heb. 9:27). These temporary healings that we should experience prepare us for the eternal healing and the redemption of our bodies at the return of Christ.

Praise the Lord, forever!

The Spiritual Gift of Giving

Romans 12:8 includes 'giving' as a spiritual gift that was part of the gift "mix" in the church at Rome. I have categorized this as a power gift because power gifts involve the active faith of the believer in the biblical promises. The gift of giving is characterized by how the giving action is done by the giver, with *no expectation of getting back the same things that were given.*

This giving is to be done with liberality. The Greek word *haplotes* can be translated: "simplicity, sincerity, uprightness, frankness, generosity, liberality ... where a man gives without letting himself be arrested by any selfish calculation ... where he gives, "without his left hand knowing what his right hand is doing" (Taken from, *Word Meanings in the New Testament,* Ralph Earl, p. 200).

Regular Christian giving is spiritual, *but it is not the spiritual gift.*

Jesus in the beatitudes declares to us the spiritual laws of the kingdom of God. He also instructs us how we who are in the world but not of the world must live in obedience to Him. Luke 6:38 reads, "give and it will be given to you: good measure, pressed down, shaken together and running over will be put into your bosom. For with the same measure that you use, it will be measured back to you." I have read where this principle has been called the law of reciprocity. All Christians should give. Regular giving activates this law of reciprocity. What is inherent in this law is that it makes us know that our giving will benefit both the receiver of our gift *and produce a benefit for us*. As the apostle Paul writes, "so let each give as he purposes in his heart, not grudgingly or of necessity; for God loves a cheerful giver. And God is able to make all grace abound toward you, that you always having all sufficiency in all things, may have an abundance for every good work" (2 Cor. 9:7). Wow, what a promise from God. But this *is not* the spiritual gift of giving.

Several Macedonian churches of the first century had several members operating in the gift of giving. Paul writes,

> Moreover, brethren, we make known to you [*to the Corinthian church in southern Greece–Achaia*] the *grace* of God bestowed upon the churches of Macedonia: [*northern Greece–Philippi, Thessalonica, Berea, etc.*] that in a great trial of affliction the abundance of their joy and their deep poverty abounded in the riches of their liberality. For I bear witness that according to their ability, yes, and beyond their ability, they were freely willing. Imploring us with much urgency, that we would receive the gift and the fellowship of the ministering to the saints. And not only as we had hoped, but they first gave themselves to the Lord, and then to us by the will of God. (2 Cor. 8:1–5)

The "gift of giving" is where the Holy Spirit prompts a believer to give of what they have sacrificially, even beyond their ability, with no expectation of repayment in kind. The only reward expected is the **joy** of the Lord, joy in the opportunity to fellowship with other saints, and joy that God will receive glory.

The gift of giving may not always be money, but it always includes *giving up with genuine joy that which is sacrificial to the believer.* Biblical examples of saints operating in the "gift of giving": Acts 4: 36, 37 (Joseph, the Cyprian Levite, aka Barnabas); 2 Corinthians 8:1–3 (individuals in the churches of Macedonia); Philippians 4:15 (individuals in the church at Philippi: Epaphroditus, Lydia); 1 Corinthians 16:17 (Stephanas, Fortunatus, and Achaicus). See also Mark 12:41–43.

What the gift of giving *is not!*

> It is not giving of your regular gifts to the church (tithes and offering.)
>
> It is not giving with the motive of getting anything back!

Do you have, or have you ever acted in the gift of giving? Have you ever obeyed a prompting to give far more that you had budgeted to the poor, your church, or a ministry? Have you ever been glad to go without so that you could give to someone or a work that God has prompted you to give to? If you have operated in this gift, or believe God is prompting you in it, share your experiences with your spiritual overseers. Ask them to pray with you and see if they agree with what you are sensing. With their encouragement, continue to pray for the Holy Spirit to lead you in the gift of giving.

The Gift of Service
(Also Translated as the Gift of Ministry)

"Having then gifts differing according to the grace that is given to us ... prophecy ... according to the proportion of faith; or ministry ... *let us wait on our* ministering" (Rom. 12:6–7 KJV). The apostle Paul continues outlining seven of the spiritual gifts operating at Rome, which is slightly different from the nine gifts mentioned in Corinth. The gift of ministry is the same as the gift of service.

The gift of service is where the Holy Spirit prompts a believer to be devoted in unselfish commitment to enable, aid, and assist others to do their ministry work, even in extreme or hazardous difficulties. Those who operate in this gifting are characterized by honest humility, a righteous lifestyle, and their determination to exalt God.

The Holy Spirit develops this gift in the believer "according to the proportion of faith" (Rom. 12:6 KJV), or, as you mature in faith, the more you and others will become aware of this gift operating in you.

The gift of service is evident in the administrative and supportive work of the deacon or deaconess. Our English word *deacon* is a transliteration of the Greek word *diakonos,* meaning "service." It means one who was an attendant, servant, ran errands, waited on tables, or performed other menial tasks (Acts 6:3). The teachings of Jesus turned the position of servant on its head, saying, "But he that is the greatest among you, shall be your servant" (Matt. 23:11 KJV). Jesus defines and pictures the gift of service as He emptied Himself of His godly prerogatives to become the Messiah, able to die for our sins.

> Who being in the form of God, thought it not robbery to be equal with God, but made himself of no reputation, and took upon Him the form of a servant and was made in the likeness of

men. And being found in fashion as a man, he humbled himself and became obedient unto death, even the death of the cross. (Phil. 2:6–8 KJV)

Here are some individuals from the Scriptures that were prompted in the gift of service: Acts 6:3–6 (The seven chosen deacons); Acts 1:3 (Luke the physician and historian); Acts 9:27, 11:26 (Barnabas); 2Timothy 1:16–18 (Onesiphorus).

Do You Have the Gift of Service?

Do you find yourself in, and happy with, a supporting role in the ministries at your church? Are you a loyal worker as unto the Lord who submits your natural learned skills, such as in financial (treasurer, bookkeeper, etc.), communication, business, building maintenance, music, and so forth, and your spiritual gifts of prayer, exhortation, or more for the ministry or church you are involved with? Have you ever considered that you should be responsible for being a friend and support for someone in a leadership position in ministry?

If you believe you have been gifted in service, pray for the Holy Spirit to confirm it to you. Ask other saints what they think of your service gift. Share with your elders your experiences and how you understand what God has gifted you in. Ask them also to pray, to see if they can agree with this gifting in your life. If so, God will allow your gift to make room for you.

Gift of Mercy

Mercy is an attribute, a character trait, of God. When God described Himself to Moses and prepared to write His laws to Israel, He declared to Moses first His mercy, saying, "And the Lord passed by before him, and proclaimed; "the LORD, the LORD God, *merciful* and gracious, long-suffering, and abundant in goodness and truth. *Keeping mercy* for thousands, forgiving iniquity and transgression and sin" (Exod. 34:6, 7 KJV).

Our English word *mercy* comes from the Hebrew word *chesed* meaning "kindness." Another Hebrew word, *racham,* meaning "to love, have pity," is also translated in English as mercy. Our word translated "mercy" as a spiritual gift (Rom. 12:7) comes from a Greek word *oiktirmos* meaning "pity, compassion, merciful."

The gift of mercy is evident when the Holy Spirit implants feelings of empathy, pity, compassion, and kindness into the spirit of a believer, allowing that believer to act in faith to forgive and even to forestall judgment and punishment that the offending person deserves.

Examples of the gift of mercy in the Scriptures: Jesus operated in the gift of mercy when He said, "Father forgive them for they know not what they do" (Luke 23:34 KJV). Deacon Stephen exhibited the gift of mercy, as the leaders of Judah were stoning him, saying, "Lord, lay not this sin to their charge" (Acts 7:60 KJV). In addition, I believe apostle Barnabas also responded through the gift of mercy to seek out Saul (later Paul), going eighty-five miles beyond the city of Antioch, Syria, to Tarsus, Cilicia (Acts 11:25), to bring Paul back to Antioch and to call Paul, after eight years, to be engaged again in the work of the ministry.

Do You Have, or Have You Operated in the Gift of Mercy?

- Have you ever been prompted by the Holy Spirit to forgive publicly and intentionally those who have done you wrong?

- Has your heart been stirred to bless the poor or homeless that you see or know who are near you?

- Do you find yourself strongly concerned and feel compassion on people being treated unjustly?

If you believe the Holy Spirit has gifted you with the gift of mercy, talk to your spiritual overseers to share with them your experiences. Ask them to pray for and with you and see if they agree and sense this gifting operating in your life. With their agreement and encouragement, pray for the Holy Spirit to give you guidance in the gift of mercy.

The Gift of Leadership

Romans 12:8 speaks of a spiritual gift of leadership and informs us that it should be operated *with diligence*. I think this gives us a hint at what the gift of leadership does.

The gift of leadership *empowers and urges the believer to take responsibility, directing, and protecting the things of God, and it* stirs the heart of the gifted believer to become focused in doing a work, as unto the Lord, with the result that others who hear of the work, or see the work, willingly follow the gifted believer's direction. The believer operating through the gift of leadership *establishes order in chaotic situations*. One important characteristic of Holy Spirit–gifted leaders is their *humility*.

Jesus counseled His disciples to know the difference in kingdom leadership and the world's brand of leadership.

> Ye know that the princes of the Gentiles exercise dominion over them and they that are great exercise authority upon them. *But it shall not be so among you* but whosoever will be great among you let him be your minister: and whosoever will be chief among you let him be your servant. (Matt. 20:25–27 KJV)

The world is always looking for "born" leaders, those they feel have the physicality, demeanor, personality, and intelligence, who can be trained in the discipline and "worldly" leadership techniques. This training *does* develop and produce leaders. Some of the leadership techniques are good for even Christian leadership, being that some help maintain organization. But secular leadership training can result with leaders who are committed to strive and fight enviously for top leadership positions and to hold on to them, dominating all others. We who comprise the body of Christ must be careful not to confuse worldly leadership guidelines with Jesus's leadership directives.

But God's, gift of leadership is given to those baptized in the Holy Spirit *to do spiritual work with and through God's people.* It is *not* based on personality, birth order, training or having high self-esteem. A "know it all," aggressive personality or the gift of gab are not qualities that the Holy Spirit deems as valuable. But the gift of leadership is imparted on those believers who respond in faith to the prompting of the Holy Spirit *to fulfill the role and responsibility of leadership when God needs them.*

The Holy Spirit gift of leadership imparts to the gifted believer the humility to seek and receive from God His wisdom, to organize, evaluate, and *develop others* to do the work of ministry.

Old Testament biblical examples of those used in the gift of leadership are Joseph, Moses, Joshua, Gideon, David, Solomon, Daniel, and Nehemiah. In the New Testament those given the gift of leadership are found in Matthew 16:18–19 (Peter); Acts 6:3.5 (the seven deacons); Acts 13:2 (Barnabas and Saul, later Paul, Acts 13:2, and Timothy and Titus).

Do You Have the Gift of Leadership?

- Have you been moved to develop your prayer life into one where you are steadfastly seeking God's will in His word and by hearing His Spirit?

- Do you find yourself concerned about doctrine and the sharing of the gospel of Jesus Christ?

- Do you conduct Bible studies in your own home with your spouse and family?

- Do others (friends, neighbors, family) follow your lead when you talk about the things of God?

- Do you have great respect of those who have spiritual oversight over you?

If you sense God implanting in you the gift of leadership, share your experience with your church overseers. Ask them to pray for you and see if they acknowledge this gifting in you. If they agree with you and acknowledge this gift operating in you, enroll in their leadership training or become a disciple trainee under one of the leaders, becoming a friend (or son or daughter) in the Lord.

The Laying On of Hands

The laying on of hands is an action fueled by biblical faith, *where God empowers the believer to transfer spiritual things that they possess to other Christians.* These spiritual things that are transferred can include such things as identity, blessing, spiritual gifts, and authority.

The Transfer of Identity

Under the law of ancient Israel, the laying on of hands allowed the beast offered in sacrifice *to be identified as the person who offered it*, allowing the sins of that person to be transferred to the beast. It is through this symbolic act we can understand Jesus's substitutional atonement for us (Lev. 1:4; John 3:16).

The laying on of hands is a foundational New Testament biblical doctrine according to Hebrews 6:2, "of the doctrine of baptisms, of laying on of hands, of resurrection of the dead, and of eternal judgment."

The Transfer of Blessings

The laying on of the hands is very ancient in its origins. Through the laying on of hands, Israel (Jacob) blessed Ephraim and Manasseh, his grandsons (Gen. 48:14). Jesus Christ too blessed children through the laying on of hands (Matt. 19:13).

The Transfer of Spiritual Gifts—Healing and Holy Spirit baptism

Our Lord Jesus established the laying on of hands to be one of the ways He transferred the healing power that was in Him upon some of those individuals that He healed. Jesus used the laying on of hands even in an atmosphere where the majority lacked faith in Him (Mark 6:5, 6). Demonic power causing sickness was broken when Jesus laid His hands on many (Luke 13:13.) The apostles Peter and John prayed and laid hands on the new believers in Samaria so they might *receive the baptism of the Holy Spirit* (Acts 8:15, 16). Holy Spirit baptism was also transferred by Paul to twelve new Christians at Ephesus (Acts 19:6). Spiritual gifts were also transferred by the apostle Paul to Timothy by the laying on of hands (1 Tim. 4:14).

The Transfer of Authority

Under the law of Moses, leadership authority was transferred from one generation to another by the laying on of hands (Num. 27:18–23). But note, in Joshua's inauguration, we see an additional outcome of the laying on of hands; a spiritual implant of wisdom is given to him: "now Joshua the son of nun was full of the spirit of wisdom, for Moses had laid his hands on him; so, the children of Israel heeded him and did as the Lord had commanded Moses" (Deut. 34:9). King David, in writing Psalm 139, declares that God transfers his protection over us through (spiritually) laying His hands on us (Ps.139:5).

Under the New Covenant, the power to transfer authority through the laying on of hands continues. The body of Christ (the local church) in the ancient city of Antioch, Syria, showed their agreement with the direction of the Holy Spirit to send out "Barnabas and Saul to the work to which I have called them" (Acts 13:2). They transferred the church's authority to "send out" apostles by the laying on of hands.

The church's authority to heal the sick among us through the prayer of faith is activated by anointing them with oil—placing their hands on them (James 5:14, 15; John 20:21–23).

The act of the laying on of hands as a spiritual gift is when the Holy Spirit prompts and infuses that faith action with the power to transfer God's spiritual things (identity, blessings, spiritual gifts, and authority) through one Christian or group of Christians to another.

Has God used you in the gifting of laying on of hands? Well, saint of God, the only way to know for sure is to pray. And, if prompted by the Holy Spirit, pray that you may transfer spiritual things you have to those you desire to see grow to that place. Start with your own family if possible. May God's blessings be with you and yours.

Let's
Summarize

CHAPTER EIGHT

SUMMATION OF THE GIFTS AND THEIR DEFINITIONS

The Revelation Gifts

1. The 'Word of Wisdom': the supernatural revealing by the Holy Spirit to the understanding of a believer of part of God's plans, purpose, and will, in the future for a person, or even a place or thing.

2. The 'Word of Knowledge': the supernatural revealing by the Holy Spirit to a believer, enabling them to know in part what God knows concerning a person, place, thing, or situation. The word of knowledge speaks to things in the present or in the past.

3. The 'Discerning of spirits': the supernatural revelation by the Holy Spirit to a believer's human spirit or mind, allowing them to perceive things in the spirit realm.

4. The 'Teaching gift': the supernatural revelation by the Holy Spirit imparting insight, understanding, and knowledge of God's intent, meaning, and mind, in sharing and explaining the holy Scriptures. The teaching gift reorients the mind of believers to obedience of Christ.

The Speaking Gifts

5. The 'Gift of Faith' enables a believer to speak God's faith, operating within the parameters of the will of God and the word of God. This gift allows a believer to speak a word without doubt and receive a miraculous result. This faith requires no action on the believer's part, only speaking.

6. The 'Gift of Tongues' enables the believer to speak in a language unknown to them enabling them to receive personal edification and worship God in "spirit and truth." Speaking in an unknown tongue can also be the initial sign of Holy Spirit baptism.

7. The 'Gift of Interpretation of Tongues' allows a believer to understand the meaning of an unknown tongue spoken aloud as a message to the congregation. The gifted believer is then able to speak that understanding, thereby interpreting the tongue that was spoken. That interpretation becomes prophecy, which is to be judged by the leaders and congregation.

8. The 'Gift of Prophecy' is where words are spoken under the unction of the Holy Spirit, in your native language, that edify, exhort, and comfort those to whom the gifted believer is speaking.

9. The 'Gift of Exhortation': the supernatural ability given by the Holy Spirit to speak the word of God with boldness, urgency, and warning. The gift allows the exhorter to give spiritual advice that encourages sanctification, repentance, and renewal in Christ Jesus and causes those being exhorted to sense that what they heard spoken was from God.

10. The 'Gift of the Working of Miracles' is in operation as the believer is prompted by the Holy Spirit to do some action, resulting in a miraculous result. The actual miracle that is done can involve anything God has created.

11. The 'Gifts of Healings' is a combination of spiritual gifts, imparted through the prompting of the Holy Spirit and faith (either biblical, with work involved, or God's faith, with only speaking and no work) that results in the healing of the body, soul, or spirit of a human, or even healing of the land or its features.

12. The 'Gift of Giving' is where the believer is prompted by the Holy Spirit to act by faith and give sacrificially some or all that they possess with no expectation of reward or repayment.

13. The 'Gift of Service' is where the Holy Spirit prompts a believer to, by faith, be devoted to unselfish commitment, enabling, aiding, and assisting others to do their ministry work, even in extreme or hazardous difficulties.

14. The 'Gift of Mercy' operates as the Holy Spirit implants feelings of empathy, pity, compassion, and kindness into the human spirit of a believer, allowing that believer to act in faith to forgive and then forestall judgment and punishment that the offending person deserves.

15. The 'Gift of Leadership' empowers and urges the believer to act by faith and take responsibility, directing and protecting the things of God. The gift imparts humility to seek and receive from God wisdom to organize, evaluate, and develop others to do the work of ministry.

16. The 'Laying on of hands" is an action fueled by biblical faith whereby God endows the believer to transfer spiritual things to other Christians.

CONCLUSION

The spiritual gifts are given to the body of Christ and are an important part of fulfilling God's plan, purposes, and direction for each individual believer's life. The spiritual gifts are a key part of our endowment with spiritual abilities that enables us to walk *in* the Spirit and fulfill our prescribed "niche" in the body of Christ. It also allows us to work and fellowship in harmoniously with other believers, and to achieve victory over the enemy until Christ's return. The spiritual gifts are *spiritual* and thus cannot be identified, defined, or exercised except by comparing spiritual things with other spiritual things. The spiritual things that we are using to compare are the prompting of the Holy Spirit, the holy Bible, the Word of God, and the agreement of our human spirit that has become spiritually alive at our salvation.

The gifts of the Holy Spirit are embedded in us at salvation, but they are released in us at our baptism in the Holy Spirit. Through the gifts, God gives us enablement (power) to worship Him in spirit and in truth, power to edify ourselves and others, and the power to see the miraculous done in Jesus name.

The gifts of the Holy Spirit are part of God's strategy to spiritually unite, supply, and grow His church. Ephesian 4 tells us, "The whole body joined and knit together by what every joint supplies according to the effective working by which every part does its share causes growth of the body"

(Eph. 4:16). The Holy Spirit has given us these spiritual gifts so that each of us have something 'spiritual' to supply to the body. When we do not know of our gifts or how to use them, we are not doing our share to grow the body.

This is not an exhaustive work. Other spiritual gifts that God has given His people may be missing here. But for those familiar in the workings of the spiritual gifts, this writing is merely reviewing 'elementary principles' of the 'spiritual things' of Christ, (Heb.6:1,2). But for those not as familiar, it is a call to know the foundation of our spiritual roots; from true salvation, to Holy Spirit baptism, adherence to the Bible (the Word of God), and walking in the supernatural aids given through our new life in Christ. These spiritual things are implanted in us to be activated by their use, empowering us to "walk after the Holy Spirit, not fulfilling the desires of our sinful nature."

This is also written to remind us of the spiritual nature of Christianity. Yet living in these last days, we must expect the enemy to cause false spirituality and false signs and wonders to arise. But we must not let the false be confused with the genuine. We must not let the proliferation of the false to restrict the spiritual work of God in His people.

According to one bank source, counterfeit money is revealed by those who see 'real' money every day. So also, will the 'real' gifts of God be shown, as they are taught, identified, and practiced in the Church services of the Body of Christ. Let's free the people of God to respond to the promptings of the Holy Spirit, under the controls of the Word of God, and the watchful eyes of Church leadership.

Regardless of the state of the world, God is still in control, fulfilling His prophetic Word to perfection. God has given us the Scripture as our control to establish what is of God and what is not, saying, "Surely the Lord God does nothing, unless He reveals His secret to His servants the prophets," and, "for Thou has magnified Thy Word above all thy Name" (Amos 3:7; Ps. 138:2 KJV).

To the praise of our Lord and Savior, Christ Jesus.

— Pastor William (Bill) Garvin,
email: bbgarvin1130@gmail.com

www.ingramcontent.com/pod-product-compliance
Lightning Source LLC
Chambersburg PA
CBHW070758120626

46557CB00002B/653